First World War
and Army of Occupation
War Diary
France, Belgium and Germany

27 DIVISION
Divisional Troops
1/2 Wessex Field Company Royal Engineers
21 December 1914 - 31 December 1915

WO95/2258/3

The Naval & Military Press Ltd
www.nmarchive.com
Published in association with The National Archives

Published by

The Naval & Military Press Ltd

Unit 10 Ridgewood Industrial Park,

Uckfield, East Sussex,

TN22 5QE England

Tel: +44 (0) 1825 749494

www.naval-military-press.com

www.nmarchive.com

This diary has been reprinted in facsimile from the original. Any imperfections are inevitably reproduced and the quality may fall short of modern type and cartographic standards.

© **Crown Copyright**
Images reproduced by permission of The National Archives, London, England, 2015.

Contents

Document type	Place/Title	Date From	Date To
Heading	WO95/2258-3		
Heading	1/2nd Wessex Fld Coy R.E. Dec 1914-Dec 1915		
Heading	2nd Wessex Field Coy, RE. Vol I 21.12.14-31.1.15		
War Diary	Winchester	21/12/1914	21/12/1914
War Diary	Harve	22/12/1914	23/12/1914
War Diary	Aire	25/12/1914	06/01/1915
War Diary	Neteren	07/01/1915	07/01/1915
War Diary	Dickebusch	08/01/1915	24/01/1915
War Diary	Zevecoten	25/01/1915	31/01/1915
Diagram etc	Appendix 2		
Heading	2nd Wessex Field Coy. RE. Vol II 1-28.2.15		
War Diary	Dickebusch	01/02/1915	15/02/1915
War Diary	Zevecoten	17/02/1915	23/02/1915
War Diary	Dickebusch	24/02/1915	28/02/1915
Heading	2nd Wessex Field Coy RE Vol III 1-31.3.15		
War Diary	Dickebusch	01/03/1915	07/03/1915
War Diary	Zevecoten	08/03/1915	13/03/1915
War Diary	Dickebusch	14/03/1915	21/03/1915
War Diary	Zevecoten	22/03/1915	31/03/1915
Diagram etc	Appendix 3		
Diagram etc	Appendix 4		
Diagram etc	Appendix 5		
War Diary		14/03/1915	16/03/1915
Heading	2nd Wessex Field Coy RE Vol IV 1-30.4.15		
War Diary	Zevecoten	01/04/1915	01/04/1915
War Diary	Zevecoten Ypres	02/04/1915	02/04/1915
War Diary	Ypres	03/04/1915	25/04/1915
War Diary	Ypres Potijze	26/04/1915	26/04/1915
War Diary	Potijze	27/04/1915	28/04/1915
Diagram etc	Appendix 6		
War Diary	Potijze	29/04/1915	30/04/1915
Operation(al) Order(s)	Operation Order No. 21 By Brig. General J.R. Longley, Commanding 82nd Infantry Brigade.	01/04/1915	01/04/1915
Heading	2nd Wessex Field Coy RE Vol V 1-31.5.15		
War Diary	Hooge	01/05/1915	04/05/1915
War Diary	Ypres	05/05/1915	27/05/1915
War Diary	Bailleul	28/05/1915	28/05/1915
War Diary	Armentiere	29/05/1915	31/05/1915
Heading	War Diary of 2nd Wessex Field Company R.E. from May 1st 1915 to May 31st 1915		
Heading	War Diary of 2nd Wessex Field Coy RE from June 1st & June 30th November		
War Diary	Armentieres	01/06/1915	30/06/1915
Heading	War Diary Of 2nd Wessex Field Company Royal Engineers T. From July 1st To July 31st Volume VII		
War Diary	Armentieres	01/07/1915	16/07/1915
War Diary	Erquinghem	17/07/1915	31/07/1915
Heading	War Diary of 2nd Wessex Field Coy R.E. From Aug 1st to Aug. 31st Inclusive Volume VIII		
War Diary	Erquinghem	01/08/1915	31/08/1915

Diagram etc	Appendix 7		
Diagram etc	Appendix 8		
Diagram etc	Appendix 9		
Diagram etc	Appendix No. 10		
Diagram etc	Appendix 11		
Heading	War Diary Of 2nd Wessex Field Company R.E. From 1st Sept 15 to 30th Sept 15 Volume IX		
War Diary	Erquinghem	01/09/1915	11/09/1915
Diagram etc	Appendix 12		
War Diary	Erquinghem	12/09/1915	16/09/1915
War Diary	Ferme La Grand Marquette	17/09/1915	19/09/1915
War Diary	Hamel	20/09/1915	20/09/1915
War Diary	Chuignolles	21/09/1915	30/09/1915
Heading	1/2 Wessex Fd Coy RE Oct 15 Vol X		
Heading	War Diary of 2nd Wessex Field Company R.E. from 1st October to 31st October 1915 Volume		
War Diary	Fontaine Le Cappy	01/10/1915	18/10/1915
War Diary	Chuignolles	19/10/1915	24/10/1915
War Diary	Mericourt	25/10/1915	26/10/1915
War Diary	Boves	27/10/1915	27/10/1915
War Diary	Saissemont	28/10/1915	31/10/1915
Heading	War Diary of 2nd Wessex Field Company R.E. from 1st November to 30th November 1915 (Volume XI)		
Miscellaneous	Officer i/c AG's Office Base	02/10/1915	02/10/1915
War Diary	Saissemont (Somme)	01/11/1915	08/11/1915
War Diary	Saissemont	09/11/1915	24/11/1915
War Diary	Saissemont (Somme)	25/11/1915	30/11/1915
Heading	War Diary of 2nd Wessex Field Coy R.E. T.F. From Dec 1st 1915 to Dec 31st 1915 Volume XII		
War Diary	Saissemont Somme	01/12/1915	08/12/1915
War Diary	Marseilles	09/12/1915	31/12/1915
Miscellaneous	Appendix 1		

W095/22583
W095/22583

27TH DIVISION
DIVL ENGINEERS

1/2ND WESSEX FLD COY R.E.

DEC 1914 — DEC 1915.

Numbered 501 from 1/2/17

157/4896

27th Division

2nd Wessex Field Coy: RE.

Vol I 21.12.14 — 31.1.15.

Diaries 2nd by RE

WAR DIARY
or
INTELLIGENCE SUMMARY.
(Erase heading not required.)

Army Form C. 2118.

Sheet 1

Instructions regarding War Diaries and Intelligence Summaries are contained in F.S. Regs., Part II and the Staff Manual respectively. Title pages will be prepared in manuscript.

HEADQUARTERS
3/5
4 APR 1915
27th DIVISION

Hour, Date, Place	Summary of Events and Information	Remarks and references to Appendices
9.15 a.m. 21/12/14 WINCHESTER	Proceeded march route to SOUTHAMPTON & embarked on S.S. Chyebassa all aboard 7 p.m.	Appendix 1. Strength of Company.
2.30 p.m. 22/12/14 HAVRE	Arrived alongside quay. Disembarkation complete 12.30 a.m. 23/12/14. Proceeded to Rest Camp No.1. Transport technical equipment deficient.	ditto
11.30 p.m. 23/12/14	Left rest camp. Entrain at Gare de Marchandises, entrainment complete 4.30 a.m.	ditto
4.0 a.m. 25.12.14 AIRE	Arrived AIRE detrainment complete 6.30 a.m. marched to billets at PONT GASSON at 7 a.m.	ditto
26.12.14	Billets at PONT GASSON. Overhauling equipment, orders received to be ready to move at short notice by 1 p.m. Order then cancelled. Reconnoitering position on line STEENBECQUE - ISBERGUES with representatives of G.H.Q. staff, Div.B.O. staff & 81 Inf.B.D.E. staff. Company ordered to march to WITTES for a return.	ditto
27.12.14	Reconnoitering position on line STEENBECQUE - ISBERGUES.	Manoeuvring to a pivot. ditto
28.12.14	ditto	ditto
29.12.14	Preparing schemes for change of troops in above position and setting up of work. Thawing up of Left Front bridges over Rivers etc. No.1 Section entrenching on E flank of CANAL.	30 men digging 30 men breaking ditto storms.
30.12.14	Damage of trenches constructed by Infantry.	90 men digging 30 men breaking 18 men consolidated.
31.12.14	Ditto.	1.20 men digging.

Army Form C. 2118.
Sheet 2

WAR DIARY
or
INTELLIGENCE SUMMARY.
(Erase heading not required.)

Instructions regarding War Diaries and Intelligence
Summaries are contained in F.S. Regs., Part II
and the Staff Manual respectively. Title pages
will be prepared in manuscript.

Hour, Date, Place	Summary of Events and Information	Remarks and references to Appendices
1-1-15. AIRE	Sappers drawing picks constructed by infantry. 6 Carpenters constructing box drains to carry trenches. 1 Joiner sent on to corner of land to carry across trenches. For Rl. preparing estimate of roofing material required for white position front line. Report sent to R/Rde Headquarters.	81 men inoculated. 30 men off sick
2-1-15. "	1 Section Sappers draining trenches. 6 Carpenters making hut doors. O.C. setting out second line with G.O.C. 91 Inf Bde. O.C. Lt Blain and representative G.H.Q. Capt. Willis preparing report for bridge across CANAL DE LA LYS 1½ mile East of AIRE. Received C in C order at 7.20 pm. to work in answer off, order No 1 given at 8.30. Move off complete at 11.30 pm. 7 Officers 130 other ranks on parade. March to BOESEGHEM & return to billets 12.45 am (3-1-15) People to late prep. cards as units had been inoculated all other vehicles taken. Sent in Rl. Belgn. estimate of material required to plank all fire trenches. Drawings of trenches for inspection of all horses, rifles etc.	40 men half day
3-1-15 "	Overhauling all harness requirement. Sent by C.R.E. order the two Carbon Wagons complete with horses Lances & harness were men NCO to report of R.E. lst Army Col. at	
4-1-15 "		
5-1-15 "	Tent mor. order given 11.0 am. moved off 12.30 pm. Route march via WITTES BLARINGHEM	

2 W Coy LV by RE

Army Form C. 2118.
Sheet 3.

WAR DIARY
or
INTELLIGENCE SUMMARY.
(Erase heading not required.)

Instructions regarding War Diaries and Intelligence Summaries are contained in F.S. Regs., Part II and the Staff Manual respectively. Title pages will be prepared in manuscript.

Hour, Date, Place	Summary of Events and Information	Remarks and references to Appendices
6 . 1 . 15 , AIRE, 9.8 am	Left AIRE marched to METEREN 23½% of coopers gunsmith & carpenters march without riding on the wagons. billeted at METEREN for the night. (marched with 87 N.Coys (Boles).)	
7 . 1 . 15 . METEREN 8.30 am	Left METEREN marched to DICKEBUSCH via BAILLEUL LOCRE WESTOUTRE RENINGHELST OUDERDOM Fine weather + 5 hours delay at OUDERDOM left OUDERDOM at 6 pm & delayed 1 hour by other motor-vehicles getting stuck on the road arrived DICKEBUSCH 8.30. Bicycles except Pte II Tashwood Qs. returned by later in the night. The coopers in gait of weather able the marched better than the way the previous day.	
8 . 1 . 15 . DICKEBUSCH	Cleaning up, & making small repairs for Sanchoro. wheeled cart for Report	
9 . 1 . 15 . "	Making javelin hurdles, repairing roads making celery at R.E. Park. Reconnoitring road of ETANG de DICKEBUSCH for roadway eitinerade trenches & return report to R.E. H.Q.D.E	
10 . 1 . 15 . "	Cutting bullet proof making hurdles & wire Collecting barrels as per C.R.E. order. Lt. Thomson reconnoitring armentieres - Bailleul for E.E. stores exp. will be remaining vicinity of DICKEBUSCH	
11 . 1 . 15 . "	One section repairing R.E. Park. Two sections making javelin hurdles one section collecting barrels & assisting R.E. store duties ½ section of trestles finished on night of 10/11 with Cpl D.M. str. Champnefs.	

Army Form C. 2118.

Sheet 4

WAR DIARY
or
INTELLIGENCE SUMMARY.
(Erase heading not required.)

Hour, Date, Place	Summary of Events and Information	Remarks and references to Appendices
12. 1. 15 DICKEBUSCH	Road improvements on OUDERDOM & VLAMERTINGHE Road. 1 Section making improvements in RR Park and making drainage round dugouts at St. ELOI. Shannon & MFQ Men made trenches at St. ELOI.	M?
13. 1. 15 "	Road widening on above road. 1 Section making various small works at the Shannon Hotel. Wales at St. ELOI. Overhauled tools at the military & received 8 lamps.	M? The military H? used as a depot, warning established for men returned from trenches
14. 1. 15 "	Road widening as above. Preparing materials for use in trenches. OC & MFQ visited trenches in Oast Fields & areas on west the Shannon. Overhauled the trenches.	M?
15. 1. 15 "	Road widening as above. Preparing materials for use in trenches. Capt Wells & Wells 1910 gan in trenches at night, clearing fire trench, planting bottom, erecting bridges &c. Report on the military & the Brewery as to availability for use as working place &c.	M? Report sent to CRE.
16. 1. 16 "	Road widening as above and preparing materials for use in trenches. Lt & Men & Walch jr finishes with 6 NCO men damming up Section of trench for removing liquid mud. OC & [?] Shannon made Reconnaissance for early morning to advance to dugouts this finish.	M?
17. 1. 15 "	Road widening. Preparing materials for RR Park & Mckay two light foot bridges. Shan Bridge used first inspection on the Curls sullen at night. Capt wells & Shannon made a survey report on all trenches in Curls Section. Capt with snap obt visited St ELOI with Maj Sutton R[?] in early morning. 18th decided on advanced position of 2 line trench	M? Report sent to OC 82[?] Bde asking for a number [?] sent to CRE

2 Wing 2nd by 18

Army Form C. 2118.

WAR DIARY
or
INTELLIGENCE SUMMARY
(Erase heading not required.)

Sheet 5

Hour, Date, Place	Summary of Events and Information	Remarks and references to Appendices
18.1.15. DICKEBUSCH.	3 Sections Road improvements as above. 1 Section Preparing materials for trenches and miscellaneous work in R.E. Park and &c in DICKEBUSCH. 2nd Lieut A. White went out to ST ELOI to supervise infantry working party digging supporting trenches. He was killed by a random bullet while engaged on this duty.	MT
19.1.15. DICKEBUSCH	3 Sections. Road improvements as above. 1 Ptoloon hy? carrying materials. 1 Section. R.E. Park and miscellaneous work in DICKEBUSCH. Lieut Mills and 12 men laying out trenches for New defensive position on line x-roads 400 x S.W. N.W. VERSTRAAT — KRUISTRAATHOEK.	MT
20.1.15 DICKEBUSCH	1 Section Road improvements as above. 1 Section R.E. Park as above. 2 Sections Clearing Brushwood on new defensive position. Capt Willis + 20 Scottish worth party of 12 men + stores to trenches at M.00N. 7 p.m. A German specimen airtorpedo in a piece of bumph reported particularly bad.	MT

2/1 Can Fld Coy RE

WAR DIARY
or
INTELLIGENCE SUMMARY.
(Erase heading not required.)

Army Form C. 2118.
Sheet 6

Instructions regarding War Diaries and Intelligence Summaries are contained in F.S. Regs., Part II. and the Staff Manual respectively. Title pages will be prepared in manuscript.

Hour, Date, Place	Summary of Events and Information	Remarks and references to Appendices
21.1.15 DICKEBUSCH	2 sections cutting brushwood in woods in second position. 1 section on improvement of roads. 1 section R.E. Park and miscellaneous work in DICKEBUSCH.	1 Officer & 15 men in hospital. 40 men attending doctor.
22.1.15 "	2 sections cutting brushwood as above. 1 section improvement of roads in morning; went out by night to launches with sandbags, boards and fascines & filled 20 feet of very muddy trench & floor 3 ins - also made parapet bullet proof and put up parados 2ft high. 1 section R.E. Park & miscellaneous work in DICKEBUSCH.	/M
23.1.15 "	2 sections - stockades in second position 1 section - R.E. Park. 1 section - R.E. Park (½day) resting after night work.	/M
24.1.15 "	Left DICKEBUSCH 9 am in column route arrived ZEVECOTEN 10.40 am. visit with Adv. Billets. Lt-Colonel R.E. joined Company on transfer from 1st Wessex Field Coy R.E. Capt Shannon R.E. attached to 5th Midland R.E. and assumed of DICKEBUSCH. Company half day sorting & carrying & carrying stores for huts. Offrs explaining sites & arranging work. NCO out to BOESCHEPE to perfect in plans required for improvements at Hospices.	/M

(73989) W4141—463. 400,000. 9/14. H.&J.Ltd. Forms/C. 2118/10.

Army Form C. 2118.

Sheet 7

WAR DIARY
or
INTELLIGENCE SUMMARY.
(Erase heading not required.)

Hour, Date, Place	Summary of Events and Information	Remarks and references to Appendices
7am to 5pm ZEVECOTEN. Jan 25th 1915.	NCO 14 men to BAILLEUL to remain for purpose of loading timber &c. 2 men to BOESCHEPE to superintend boilers. 1 Carpenter (NCO) to Hospital BOESCHEPE assist in C.E. work. 1 NCO 16 men loading & unloading Parties of an 3 field Coys R.E. on arrival ZEVECOTEN. 1 Officer to BAILLEUL to reconnoitre for R.E. stores & arrange wagon loading details. 1 Subaltern to POPERINGHE to reconnoitre for R.E. Stores. 3 Officers 54 men knitting.	APPENDIX 2. Typing hut 3 huts for 30 men hutt complete 2 " finished off 1 " skirted/papered :1 1 " " :3 1 " " :4 1 " :6 To date 1 Officer 22 men in hospital, general debility due to exceeding skill of country.
7am to 5pm ZEVECOTEN. Jan 26. 1915.	Details as for 25th. 1 NCO 16 men to DICKEBUSCH & damm ditan near Brewery. 1 NCO 16 men prepared ball against first position. Zevecoten. Working all Sir Coln's huts at ZEVECOTEN. Remainder of Coy 167 " knitting, building, taking frames	P.H. H. 4 huts built. A. Collecting frames & huts vacated.
7am to 5pm Jan 27. 15 25 V & CO TEN	Details same as for 26th. 1 Salvn (30 men) road widening on WESTOUTRE - RENINGHELST Road by civilians on similar work. Remainder of Company knitting	70* employing timber of manwork on road felled 30* near Ordnance road. H. 1 hut built.

Army Form C. 2118.

Sheet 8

WAR DIARY
or
INTELLIGENCE SUMMARY.
(Erase heading not required.)

Instructions regarding War Diaries and Intelligence Summaries are contained in F.S. Regs., Part II. and the Staff Manual respectively. Title pages will be prepared in manuscript.

Hour, Date, Place	Summary of Events and Information	Remarks and references to Appendices
Jan 28. ZEVECOTEN	1 Section road widening & 50 civilians hutting 3 " " Other details as for 27th	120' corduroy road laid + 90' covered with rubble 4.2 huts built. M
Jan 29 "	1 Section road widening & 50 civilians hutting 3 Section hutting Other details as for 28th	85' corduroy road laid 120' rubble covered 3 huts built. M
Jan 30 "	1 Section road widening & 45 civilians 3 Section hutting Small details as for 29th. 1 Officer on road report. 4th Company Cox Cable & R.E. Section Left ZEVECOTEN	3 huts built 1 Q (woman)hut built 1 Q " 1 Q 2 M
Jan 31st 5 a.m. 6.40 a.m. 1 p.m. & 5 p.m.	Arrived SHIPPENBERG BEEK, billets at same. Employ Atelier of Carpenters & 20 pioneers at civil position during night. 18 Officer & 12 were superintending civilian working parties on 2nd	85' corduroy road built. M

(signature)

2 Wessex Fld Coy RE

APPENDIX 2.
TEMPORARY HUTS.

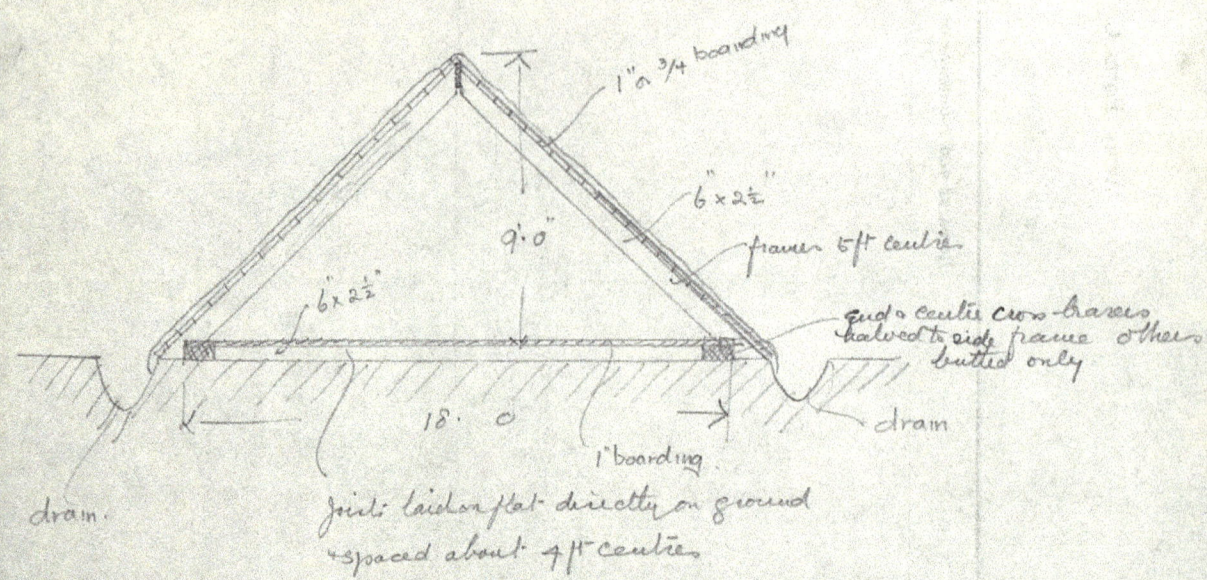

One end boarded in with apex of triangle fitted with movable shutter for ventilation & other end with doorway & loose door secured as desired with wood turn buckles.

Length of hut & suit No of men.   30 ft long for 30 men
                                                            40 ft -- 40

Covering either tarred felt or tarpaulin secured with thin battens on top. Tarred felt if available to be preferred as apex ventilation could then be arranged as sketch

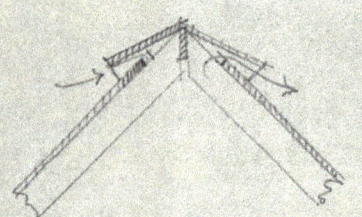

Peter G. Fy

151/4896

29th Division

2nd Wessex Field Coy. RE.

Volume 1 — 28.2.15

2nd Wessex Field Coy R.E.

Army Form C. 2118.

HEADQUARTERS
316
4 APR. 1915

WAR DIARY
or
INTELLIGENCE SUMMARY.
(Erase heading not required.)

Sheet 9.

Instructions regarding War Diaries and Intelligence Summaries are contained in F.S. Regs., Part II. and the Staff Manual respectively. Title pages will be prepared in manuscript.

Hour, Date, Place	Summary of Events and Information	Remarks and references to Appendices
Feb 1st DICKEBUSCH	1 Section road improvement, road HALLEBAST to OUDERDOM 14 Civilians employed Cpl. 1 Section erecting gun stand position 2 " Building shelter in woods nr. SWARTEBUSCH 1 Officer & others & engineers civilian working party on stores at night (10 civilians)	53" road completed 5 shelters constructed
Feb 2nd "	4 men + OBSERVATORY Preparing table etc ready for saw tackle 1 Section erecting 2nd line positions 1 " road improvements in wood 2 " shelters Detail leaving timber etc by Carpenters & Plumbers at PENNINGHURST 1 Officer 13 NCOs supervising civilian working parties & discipline.	6 shelters complete 4 2nd line shelters Py.
Feb 3rd "	2 Section on shelters 2 " Road making at farm BELGIUM sheet 28 NW, H.23.A NE 8 men Preparing portable entanglement 1 Officer & men supervising civilian working parties on 2 lines (110 civilians)	16 shelters constructed Total shelters in wood 30 Py
Feb 4th "	8 " Building shelter. 1 section forming road way at farm near shelter - cookery rooms 10ft wide Pick Burying cable burying cable for cookery at Cottage. Supervising cable for cookery at Offices of men supervising civilian working party on 2nd line position 15 wheel carts fetched for loading work 1 Section Building huts for Coy men in No 1 DICKEBUSCH 1 " " fresh hangars, hutting support - shelters.	3 shelters built Pd [?] 3.3" road laid, 7 yard metalled
Feb 5th "	2 " " " " " " " " " & men preparing Hurdling shelter for huts Wood shelters	Gate boarded, two frames house level & coffee cart Hangars for 2 sheds & growth well 180' & all shelters fireplaces [?] raised roof, horsham access Py

(73989) W4141-463. 400,000. 9/14. H.&J. Ltd. Forms/C. 2118/10.

Army Form C. 2118.

Sheet No.

WAR DIARY
or
INTELLIGENCE SUMMARY.
(Erase heading not required.)

Instructions regarding War Diaries and Intelligence Summaries are contained in F. S. Regs., Part II. and the Staff Manual respectively. Title pages will be prepared in manuscript.

Hour, Date, Place	Summary of Events and Information	Remarks and references to Appendices
Feb. 6th near Stokenbosch	1 Section getting huts 1 " fixing up horses lines etc & Battery Headquarters 2 " on Roadway 5 men preparing sleeping huts 1 Officer reconn. for 2 new position at night	1.
Feb 7 "	5 men cutting plates 1'.0 cwt 9 making handles 15" x 2.8" as ploughshares 12 completed 1 NCO 70 men leveling & house leading carts 1 Section building cook shelter 2 " building huts 1 Officer + 24 men improving roadway to 2nd new position at night	
Feb 8th "	1 Section erecting cook shelter 2 " " erecting huts 1 " leveling + horse + road repair 1 NCO + 4 men at R.E. Park 2 Section in trenches by 16. 19 repairing parapets + traverses. 2 men in Batt H.Qtrs on constructing cellar dug out + 2 men in dugout near S9 + 4 men in S12 building overhead cover	
Feb 9th "	1 Section hutting, 1 section on R.E. Park, on roads leading up to camp. 1 Section on trench work. work in trenches 16. 19 + 21 + dugouts + S12.	

2nd Wessex Field Coy RE

Army Form C. 2118.

WAR DIARY
or
INTELLIGENCE SUMMARY.
(Erase heading not required.)

Sheet 11

Hour, Date, Place	Summary of Events and Information	Remarks and references to Appendices
Feb 10th nr. STEENBOSCH	1 Section hutting 1 section constructing RR Rack, on roads breaking up houses Curran Camp in grounds. 2 Section on knocking of eight work wheelers 18.19.21.22. Manned St Willa out Coy. Reconnoitred road ST ELOI & MESSINES. reported there was no knocked except the Louvain station.	MK
Feb 11th	1 Section hutting 1 Section on work on RR Rack, on breaking up houses, etc. 2 section in trenches work on 16.18.19.21	MK
Feb 12th	Hdqrs Coy moved out Huts at STEENBUSCH work detail as on 11th. 2 Section in trenches 16.18.19.21 & Main tunnelling moved at ST ELOI. Unsuccessful attempt Steenwerck road ST ELOI - MESSINES. Two lorry noted.	MK
Feb 13th	Remainder of Coy moved into Huts at STEENBOSCH. Detail as on 11th. 2 section in trenches 16.18. 19.21. Placed sewn road ST ELOI MESSINES. 2 Coy to put up wire in trenches 21 during day 9 14 to observe & report on feasibility of during gap head against German pops.	MK
Feb 14th	Work in RR Rack heavy road as on Feb 11th. 2 Section prepared 6 pr trenches at night but - were stopped as enemy was expected. There when finished 19.20.21.22. 88"askel for 2 Officers female party cap walked south of 2 am RR Rack. Cap walked for officers party to arrival of Cameron on 9.12.	MK

WAR DIARY or INTELLIGENCE SUMMARY

Army Form C. 2118.

2nd Wess: Fd Coy R.E.

(Erase heading not required.)

Instructions regarding War Diaries and Intelligence Summaries are contained in F.S. Regs., Part II. and the Staff Manual respectively. Title pages will be prepared in manuscript.

Sheet 12.

Hour, Date, Place	Summary of Events and Information	Remarks and references to Appendices
BIKSCHOTE. Feb 15	At 3.10 am Coy received orders to turn out and move to TOO R.N.E. 21/S.E./2. *Coy left STUEBOSCH about 4.30 proceeded to WOORMEZEELE. 21.2.3.74. Sections sent forward to trenches reached 20.21. 22. & repaired parapet & re-rivetted. & renewed sand bags. No.2 Officer of D.Coy recommended in front of No.21 trench the enemie forward trench retired opposite to parallel. Arrived back Coy at BILLETS. No.1 Section at work on S.12 until shelled out then at work on putting improving the existing defence of VOORMEZEELE and in ground do to defence of VOORMEZEELE. Corpl. WILLIS wounded in carrying a wounded officer from communication trench at 20. and was killed in doing so. Sapper signaller & Corpl WILLIS reported missing & probably killed. No.1 can reported missing & probably killed. Section left trenches at nightfall & returned to BILLETS rehearsed to ZEVECOTEN.	1 Man wounded. Corpl WILLIS noble attempt to carry a wounded officer to safety in daylight & open ground. Open to view of the enemy within 100 yards. P/K P/K
Feb 16	Left Billets at 1 pm moved to ZEVECOTEN	
ZEVECOTEN Feb 17th	1 Section sent to Huts near HAMERTINGH to complete same. 1 Section handed to Section Commander for inspection, resting at Remainder at work on shelters in wood on ZEVECOTEN S.N. left CLYTTE wood. Received orders at 1.30 for 3 Section stand to came ready to move off at 7 & gave received orders that these would be unharnessed, but Coy ready to move at easy moment.	P/K
ZEVECOTEN Feb 18	Received orders at 5.30 am to fall in ready to move off. At 8.30 am orders to resume ordinary work. 1 Section sent to work on Cook shelters. HULS KAPPELLE huts, the Section handed to Section officer for inspection. 3 following Coys i.e. VLAMERTINGH) on huts Commander 2d Coy an 17th	3 Huss enlarged & 7 relieved & very hostile Section.

(73989) W4141—463. 400,000. 9/14. H.&J.Ltd. Forms/C. 2118/10.

Army Form C. 2118.

WAR DIARY
or
INTELLIGENCE SUMMARY.
(Erase heading not required.)

2/1st Kent R.E.

Sheet 13.

Instructions regarding War Diaries and Intelligence Summaries are contained in F.S. Regs., Part II. and the Staff Manual respectively. Title pages will be prepared in manuscript.

Hour, Date, Place	Summary of Events and Information	Remarks and references to Appendices
ZEWECOTEN Feb. 19	1 NCO & 4 men erecting cook shelter near Coy Shelter MILLEKAPELLE. 1 Section handed to Sector Commander for inspection & lathing at 1 section on huts near VLAMERTINGHE. 1 Carpenter in R.E. workshop. Remainder of Coy building huts in wood near ZEVECOTEN.	4 men received from Regiment Shelter Beaconsfield.
ZEVECOTEN Feb. 20	1 Section at work on huts near VLAMERTINGHE. 1 Section handed to Sector Commander for inspection, lathing etc. 6 Carpenters in R.E. workshop. 1 NCO & 4 men erecting shelter MILLEKAPELLE. Remainder of Coy on building huts in wood near ZEVECOTEN. 2 Horses taken ill.	P/F
ZEVECOTEN Feb. 21.	1 section at work on huts near VLAMERTINGHE. 1 section handed to Sector Commander for inspection & lathing etc. 4 Carpenters in R.E. workshop. 1 wagon bringing sheet RENINGHELST. Remainder of Coy on building huts in wood.	2 Horses shot. P/F
ZEVECOTEN Feb. 22.	1 Section building huts near VLAMERTINGHE. 4 men in camp. Sink floor in Drying Shed RENINGHELST. 3 men still in Dering shed & making some wood clips from road to Beach. Remainder on huts in Wood.	P/F
ZEVECOTEN Feb. 23.	2 Sections building huts in wood near ZEVECOTEN until 11am. 1 Section at erecting huts stable shelter shot near VLAMSK. TIMOTHE. 1 gun Coy moved to shelter DICKEBUSCH. arrived 2.30pm. Preparing work for shelter trenches.	P/F

2nd Wessex Field Co. R.E.

WAR DIARY
or
INTELLIGENCE SUMMARY.
(Erase heading not required.)

Army Form C. 2118.

Sheet 14

Instructions regarding War Diaries and Intelligence
Summaries are contained in F.S. Regs., Part II.
and the Staff Manual respectively. Title pages
will be prepared in manuscript.

Hour, Date, Place	Summary of Events and Information	Remarks and references to Appendices
DICKEBUSCH 24.2.15	Work in 1st line trenches night 23/24th Feb. NCO & 70 men revetting coves 14 Continuing work already started. NCO 4 " Sapping out from 10 NCO 12 " revetting out of R2 NCO 8 " putting overhead head-cover R1 OC & Capt Shannon with photographer 9.10.11.12 and carpenters and at Vierstraat 60ft infront of advanced listening 9 & 10. Also No.9 & R2 and in conjunction with OC tunnellers reached out to tunnel noplan 11. 1 Section in RE Park preparing Knife rests & sorting stores for Vierstraat. Finishing floor of MORTIMER. – Lt Capt Bay. 11st Artisans Commencement. [signature] P.R.C.	14 June afternoon The Colonel inspecting position
25.2.15	Work in 1st line trenches night 24/25th Feb. Started up from Trench 10. NCO 410 men revetting on new 14 Revetting trench parados emplacement in Vierstraat Wire round R1 Netting Continuing R2. revetting with wire stakes Capt Shannon in trenches 3.4 R4 "S2 reconoiting for parados for during 24th 111 Hill 60 & Zurneden # 18.10.11.12 to R.E. assistance O.C. with Hill Co6 g. wire from 9 to 10 to improvise guns in state of defence Suggested 1 Section on day work in RE Park 1 " a Hospital hut etc	[signature] R.R.

WAR DIARY or INTELLIGENCE SUMMARY

Army Form C. 2118.

3rd Wessex Field Coy R.E.

Sheet No.

Hour, Date, Place	Summary of Events and Information	Remarks and references to Appendices
Dickebusch 26.2.15	1 Section in R.E. Park. 1 Section erecting Hospital Hut. Aigle work 25/26 Feb. Sapping from 10 P.M. Continuing work in R2 & 10. 2 teen erecting at S3.	Sgt Burgess Wounded.
Dickebusch 27.2.15	1 Section in R.E. Park. 1 Section preparing approach from Sand Road round Etang de Dickebusch to revetment for 2 line position. Supporting curtain between 2 parades. Nightwork 26/27 Feb. Sapping from 10 P.M. Repairing pumps in S3 & S4. Repairing dugout S3. Continuing work in R2 & 10. Preparing site for new shelter in wood & many S3 to be constructed.	P/Foy
Dickebusch 28.2.15	1 Section constructing bridges on new road from Dickebusch - Vierstraat Road out Dickebusch La Clytte Road to cross roads 1 mile S. of H. in Dickebusch (map Belgium 1/40,000). 1 Section on new road S.W. of Etang de Dickebusch. Night work 27/28 Feb. Differ 35 ft total length. Sapping work in 10. Erecting splinter proof dug out in wood back of S3. Continuing R.2 revetting & building breastwork.	Casualties todate 5.3. Strength of Coy at date 6 officers 159 other ranks 1 interpreter 10 horses short of Establishment

P/Foy

121/5266

29th Division

2nd Wessex Field Coy: RE

Vol III 1 — 31.3.15

2ND WESSEX FIELD COY RE

Army Form C. 2118.

Sheet 18.

WAR DIARY
or
INTELLIGENCE SUMMARY.

(Erase heading not required.)

Instructions regarding War Diaries and Intelligence
Summaries are contained in F. S. Regs., Part II.
and the Staff Manual respectively. Title pages
will be prepared in manuscript.

Hour, Date, Place	Summary of Events and Information	Remarks and references to Appendices
MARCH 1st 1915 STORMEZEELE	At work on new Road as on 28th Feb. 4 works in Hospital Hut. Nightwork 1 Oft 1 March. Finished one splinter proof Shelter at Battery S 3 & started another. Continuing caps in 10 now 5 feet long. Continuing redoubt 2. Found caps from 4 impossible & suggested starting from communication trench S 2 & 3.	2 bridges ready for chenery on page 25ft wide & for foot traffic & foot them down. see appendix 3
March 2 1915 "	Work on new Road as at yesterday Work on Hospital Hut in RE Park. Nightwork 10 1/2 hours. Continuing caps in 10. Commenced drain for new caps from communication trench S 2 & 3. Finished new trench at 10. Returning slewed post & P. Continuing R 2. Continuing shelter behind S3.	7 Horses very rough road from few carts got stuck generally a poor lot.

WAR DIARY or INTELLIGENCE SUMMARY

(Erase heading not required.)

Army Form C. 2118.

Sheet 17

3 Wessex Field Coy R.E

Hour, Date, Place	Summary of Events and Information	Remarks and references to Appendices
March 3. 1915 Dickenbusch	Continuing road work as on 2nd March. Struck D. G.O.s dug out DICKEBUSCH. Made box drains for same. Night work 2/3 March. Continuing R.2. Continuing shelter behind S.3. Revetting fire trench at S3. Continuing sap no 10. Cutting thro' Wiener for sap in com trench S2 to S3. D'mills at Mound ST E101 & setting for indication of mining. Moon covered night's work. Report sent to CRE.	25 Cavalry Reg. Working. See appendix 4. 15 Infantry. 4/4/4/
March 4. 1915 "	Roads in road as above complete except chessing (none available). Hospital hut finished except for one door. Doors removed from old shelled house VOORHEZEELE & pur. Repn purchased 3/4/. Continuing G.O.s Dug out. Night work 3/4 March. Continuing R.2. Saps no 10 & sap from com trench S2 – 3. Recovering parts of o. Re-sort lining of down trench 9-10 bencher relaxies. Infantry party on same.	20 Infantry on R2. Ted Batt'n prime men thompion excellent furlough. 25 Cavalry Reg. 4/4/4

WAR DIARY or INTELLIGENCE SUMMARY

Army Form C. 2118.

2nd Mining Field Coy. R.E.

Sheet 10

(Erase heading not required.)

Hour, Date, Place	Summary of Events and Information	Remarks and references to Appendices
March 5. 1915 Dickebusch	Continuing G.O.C. dug out. Difficulty with soil which is very wet + continually falling in. Roof started. Box drains complete. Night-work H/S. Place. Continuation of R2. Boys in 10 days use 3 rebates at Group B. also returning S. Capt Shannon & 10 men started preparing for my boards dear 21. Damage again repaired from fire + attention.	25 Infantry. 2 shellers complete and one half finished.
March 6. 1915 "	Work on G.O.C. dug out. Preparing work for trenches. Continuing dugouts 10 + 3. 2 Section left billets at 5 p.m. with 10 Infantry carrying party. O.C. + Capt Shannon which in advance to recce. 3 trips by rescue were as to work necessary. S. Willis with sappers + carrying party remained at VOORMEZEELE. Rang up trench have seen Stewed & trenches 19 + 22 new 21. trenches trevour parapets finished to have been damaged by enemies shellfire. Found parapet little damaged + repaired. Came along bund where necessary. Enemy very alert. Several outbursts of rapid fire & fires. Morning received during the night. O.C. went round parties with O.C. 3 N.R. obtained whether hostility both enemies reports between Nos 21 + 22 be there. Thought it was a relation of sanders supplying at present. Arrived in billets 6.30 a.m.	P.K.

Army Form C. 2118.

SHEET 19

2ND WESSEX FIELD CO. R.E.

WAR DIARY
OR
INTELLIGENCE SUMMARY.
(Erase heading not required.)

Instructions regarding War Diaries and Intelligence Summaries are contained in F.S. Regs., Part II. and the Staff Manual respectively. Title pages will be prepared in manuscript.

Hour, Date, Place	Summary of Events and Information	Remarks and references to Appendices
March 7 1915. DICKEBUSCH	1. Section on construction of G.O.C.'s dug outs. preparing pageant etc.	2nd Infantry Brigade.
1 p.m.	Marched from STONEYSTON via HULL CORNER to ZEVECOTEN. Being relieved by 1st Wessex Field Co. R.E.	
2.30.	Arrive ZEVECOTEN + start with Hut shelters.	P/M
MARCH 8 1915. ZEVECOTEN.	2 Sections detailed to set got near huts near CANADA INN on the OUDERDOM - HALLEBAST Road. Timber for framing cut. Plentiful. One hut erected. Remainder of Sappers instruction in Sapping during morning and explosions during afternoon. Lecture by Capt Heather R.G.A. to Mounted NCO's on Stable duties and horse management. General overhaul of technical equipment + harness etc. Erection of Shelter in woods. HUTS CAPBLE	Set for 5 officer huts 2/L, Woman huts P/M
MARCH 9 "	1½ Sections building Huts near CANADA INN. ½ Section off duties. Remainder Practice in Sapping and erecting washing huts etc at shelter in wood ZEVECOTEN - LACLYTTE Road.	P/M
MARCH 10 "	1½ Sections building Huts as above. ½ Section off duties. Remainder practice in Sapping	P/M

Army Form C. 2118.

SHEET 20.

2ND WESSEX FIELD COY. R.E.

WAR DIARY
or
INTELLIGENCE SUMMARY.
(Erase heading not required.)

Instructions regarding War Diaries and Intelligence Summaries are contained in F.S. Regs., Part II. and the Staff Manual respectively. Title pages will be prepared in manuscript.

Hour, Date, Place	Summary of Events and Information	Remarks and references to Appendices
MARCH 11. ZEVECOTEN	1½ Sections hutting at CANON INN. 1 Section off duty. Remainder parades in Coyping.	
MARCH 12. "	1½ Section hut building CANON INN. 1 Section off duty. Remainder parades in Coyping making feed boxes & erecting hay racks at stables etc.	p/w
MARCH 13. " 10 am	Company marched from billets to DIXMBUSCH to relieve 1st & 5th MIDLAND Field Coys. on left Section arrived billets in Fes 11 am. Preparing for work on 1st line. Capt Willis issued a [?] to accompany unit of DIXMBUSCH. Filled in holes on road [?] DIXMBUSCH - YPRES road to KRONSTRAATHOEK	Bivo 3. LD Horses from BOESCHOPE. No 6 Mob Vety Sect. p/w
MARCH 14. DIXMBUSCH	Night work 13/14 March. Sapping out. Sapping out from left of 19 Kronda German Saps head. " Ascending in drainage work at rear of S.9. " Cutting new trench to treatment from reply 19a ft run. About 20 yds in rear of 19. Preparing scheme for putting STECON in state of defence.	

2nd WESSEX FIELD COY RE.

Army Form C. 2118.

SHEET 22

WAR DIARY
or
INTELLIGENCE SUMMARY.
(Erase heading not required.)

Instructions regarding War Diaries and Intelligence Summaries are contained in F.S. Regs. Part II. and the Staff Manual respectively. Title pages will be prepared in manuscript.

Hour, Date, Place	Summary of Events and Information	Remarks and references to Appendices
Night of 16/17 March	Capt. Long superintended setting out & erection of new breastwork running from old Breastwork to Shono trenches 19 rigs towards village of ST ELOI	Engineers were old while superintending work on 2nd Line
16.3.15 — 3.30 pm	Lt. Adems RE and 1 Coy Canterburies visited work on cutting new trench S.11. to BOIS-TIGES. About 80 yds trench practically completed when the position was shelled & work stopped. C.R.E. will see 2nd Div inspected new trench temp contracted at support trench East of the ST ELOI — YPRES Road	P.H.
MARCH 17. 7.30 am DICKEBUSCH	N⁰ Jr 2 sections under Lt Cory proceeded under C.R.E. orders to ZEVECOTEN.	
4.0 pm	Two Sections of 56th Field Coy arrived at our billets under Lt. Woods with Capt BRODIE North Midland Div Engrs attached Night work 17/18th. Two sections putting up ST ELOI in a state of defence under Capt Long R.E. of with C.R.E. inspected new support trenches being constructed East of the ST ELOI — VOORMEZEELE Road.	P.H.
March 18.	Two sections 56 Field Coy & 2 sections 2 Wessex Ploy. EOST at work on defence of ST ELOI and trenchwork on Inspected of Major Evans RE O/C of 56 Field Coy arrived village.	PH.y
March 19.	Two sections 56 Field Coy & 2 Sections 2 Wessex Field Coy at work on defence of ST ELOI.	P.H.y

Army Form C. 2118.

2nd WESSEX FIELD COY. R.E.

SHEET 23

WAR DIARY
or
INTELLIGENCE SUMMARY.
(Erase heading not required.)

Instructions regarding War Diaries and Intelligence Summaries are contained in F.S. Regs., Part II. and the Staff Manual respectively. Title pages will be prepared in manuscript.

Place	Hour, Date	Summary of Events and Information	Remarks and references to Appendices
DICKEBUSCH	March 20. 15.	2 Sections so far by, 1 Section 2nd Wessex Fd Coy on defences of ST.ELOI. 1 Section 2nd Wessex Fd Coy R.E. at work in R.E. park during day, preparing prefabs etc. & materials for nights work	BWay
DICKEBUSCH	March 21. 15	Headquarters & 2 Sections 2nd Wessex Fd Coy + 2 sections 5th Wessex Fd Coy proceeded to ZEVECOTEN at 12.30 p.m. - will not field Coy H.Q. Colonel General from C.R.E. to be prepared to move at ½ hour notice. 2 Sections proceeded for ZEVECOTEN — 2 Wessex Battalion 2 Sections proceeded for ZEVECOTEN to DICKEBUSCH & worked night on defences of ST ELOI. General overhaul of equipment etc. at ZEVECOTEN. The two sections of by 2 sections at DICKEBUSCH at work on defences of ST ELOI and clearing of trenches etc. Orders from CRE to be prepared to move at short notice.	Appendix, plans of defences of ST ELOI on 21.3.15 BWay BWay
ZEVECOTEN	March 22nd		BWay
ZEVECOTEN	March 23	2 Sections at DICKEBUSCH proceeded to ZEVECOTEN & joined Company.	BWay
ZEVECOTEN	March 24	The company proceeded to STEENBOSCH for day's work on GHQ line. Left DICKEBUSCH at 2 p.m. & returned ZEVECOTEN arriving 6.30 a.m. 25/3/15	BWay

2nd WESSEX FIELD COY. R.E.

WAR DIARY
or
INTELLIGENCE SUMMARY.

Army Form C. 2118.

SHEET 24

Hour, Date, Place	Summary of Events and Information	Remarks and references to Appendices
ZEVECOTEN March 25	2 Section proceeded DICKEBUSCH 4.30 pm for work on G.H.Q. line	25/3/4
" March 26	2 Section proceeded DICKEBUSCH 9.0 pm for similar work. Capt BUSS posted to Company	26/3/4
" March 26	Coy at rest + general overhaul of arms & equipment	26/3/4
" March 27th	2 Section at work on G.H.Q. line (first one relief)	27/3/4
" March 28	2 " " " " " " (second relief)	28/3/4
" March 29	Coy paraded at O/C disposal	29/3/4
" March 29	Sappers at work on G.H.Q. line at night in two reliefs	29/3/4
" March 30	Coy at O/C disposal	30/3/4
" March 31st	Whole Coy at work on G.H.Q. line. Left billets 7.30 pm arr work 9.0 pm aged 1st 2 Section busy up form 2 Section sappering in revetting entanglements & stair communication Finish off up	31/3/4

WAR DIARY
or
INTELLIGENCE SUMMARY.

(Erase heading not required.)

Army Form C. 2118.

APPENDIX 3.

Hour, Date, Place	Summary of Events and Information	Remarks and references to Appendices

SHELTERS behind S.B.

PLAN.

NOT TO SCALE

SECTION.

Shelters screened by planting branches all round 4 or 5 ft.

This splendid proof has been found to be suitable & comfortable & easily screened in a wood.

WAR DIARY
or
INTELLIGENCE SUMMARY.

Army Form C. 2118.

Appendix 4

(Erase heading not required.)

Instructions regarding War Diaries and Intelligence Summaries are contained in F.S. Regs., Part II. and the Staff Manual respectively. Title pages will be prepared in manuscript.

Hour, Date, Place	Summary of Events and Information	Remarks and references to Appendices
Dug out for G.O.C.	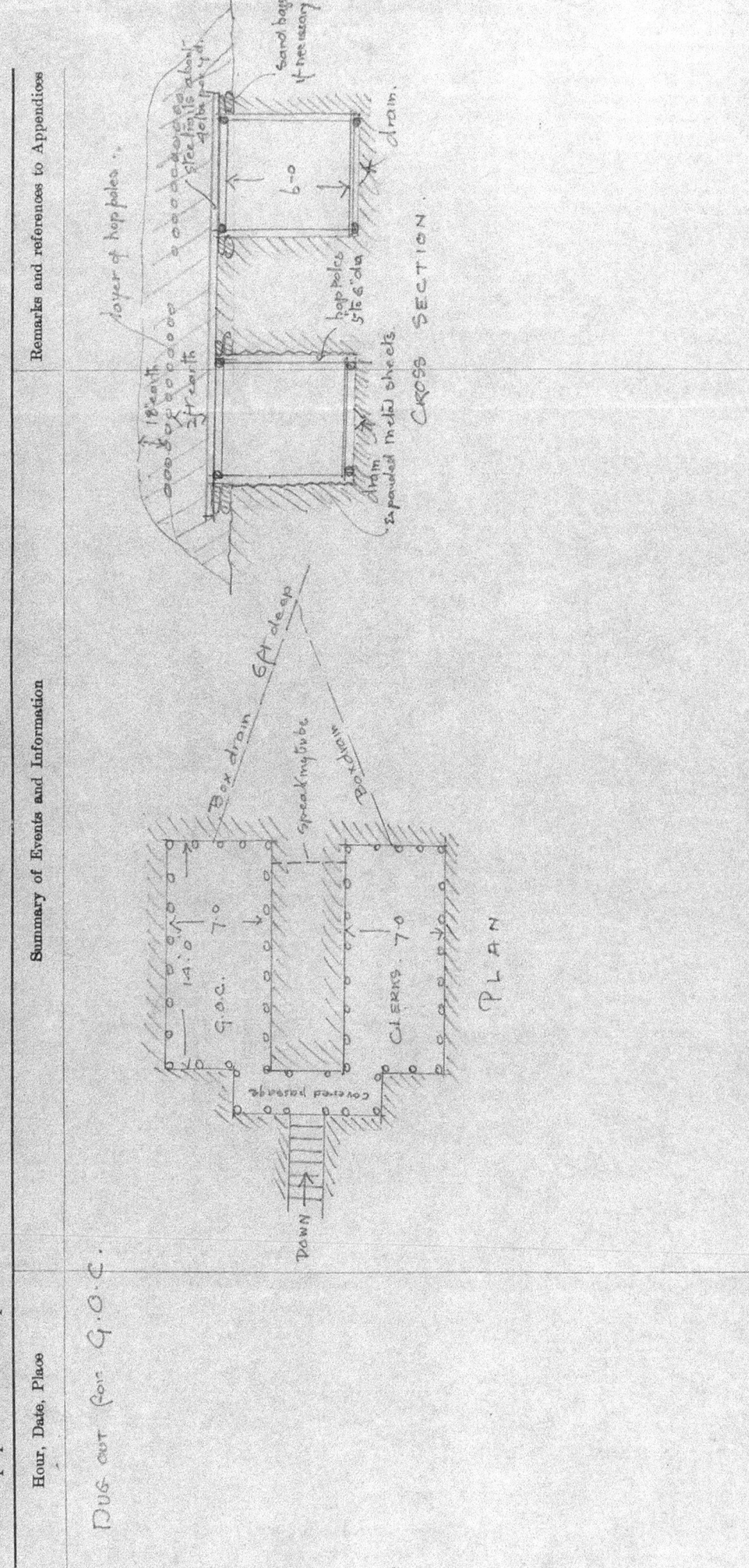	

APPENDIX 5.

SKETCH PLAN of defences of Village of ST ELOI on March 21st

NOTE
Wiring Completed : xxxx
" erected : ......
Breastwork completed
" "   not erected

2ND WESSEX FIELD COY R.E.   WAR DIARY or INTELLIGENCE SUMMARY.   Army Form C. 2118.

SHEET 21

Hour, Date, Place	Summary of Events and Information	Remarks and references to Appendices
MARCH 14 4pm	Arrangements for night work cancelled owing to heavy bombard-ment & German attack on ST-ELOI. Received orders to move Sappers to VOORMEZEELE. OC proceeded in advance, and received instructions from BRIGADIER 2/2 Inf. Bde.	
Night of March 14/15	Two sections proceeded to improve immediate defences of VOORMEZEELE. 2 Coy CAMBRIDGESHIRE TERRITORIALS placed at working party to improve & lengthen trenches S.11 - S.12. Owing to want of tools & congested state of roads this work was not started until early morning. Capt. C.M. WILLS wounded in leg about 2 am 15 March.	p/14
MARCH 15 5pm	White Coy (Sappers) proceeded to VOORMEZEELE in accordance with orders of GSOE. 2 Sections under Capt Shannon proceeded to ST ELOI & started putting village in a state of defence. Erected bullet proof barricades across road ST ELOI - YPRES. One section & one platoon Suff. Infantry improving S.11 - one section & one platoon Duty improving S.12. Extension of S.11 worked out as far as the BOLLAERTBEEK.	Capt. Ling R.E. from 1st Div R.E. attached Pmt. p/14
MARCH 16 1915 9pm 16/17	2 Sections proceeded to ST ELOI at 7 p.m. work done night Obstacle erected in front of Barricade, machine gun emplacement built. Tambours erected in front & back of defended house on N/W of ST ELOI - YPRES Road (completed). Infantry (R.S.L.) also loopholing houses & erecting Tambours across ST ELOI - VOORMEZEELE Road.	p/14

121/5314

29th Division

2nd Wessex Field Coy R.E.

Vol XIV 1 — 30.4.15.

2ND WESSEX FIELD COY R.E.

Army Form C. 2118.

WAR DIARY
or
INTELLIGENCE SUMMARY.
(Erase heading not required.)

Sheet 25.

Place	Hour, Date	Summary of Events and Information	Remarks and references to Appendices
ZEVECOTEN	1st April 1915	1 section marking out G.H.Q. 3rd Line. Remainder packing vehicles etc preparatory to move orders for following day.	
ZEVECOTEN / YPRES	2nd April 1915	Company moved by march route SOBERDORT – VLAMERTINGHE to YPRES on 82nd Inf. Bde. Company rested during day.	
YPRES	3rd April 1915	4 Officers visited new trenches – working till morning. Nos 3 & 4 Sections went out at dusk upsiding and thickening parapets in trenches. Nos 1 & 2 sections preparing materials and sorting stores in R.E. Park.	No gravel had been somewhat damaged by minenwerfer bombs.  Major Toy left in afternoon for Steenplaere (inadequate, relieved for 4th)
YPRES	4th April 1915	Continued reconnaissance of trenches. 1 Section in R.E. Park – Detachment to No 50 arranged by night to continue repairs	
YPRES	5th April 1915	Major NORTON-GRIFFITHS noted visiting area. 2 sections by day to Rigaud – Cailea Sector "thickening" parapets etc Newpany filled up near HdQrs. Canal Sector. Detachment by night thickening parapets etc. Left Section	"Shelf" scheme of thickening parapets (general idea being to save sandbags)

2ND WESSEX FIELD COY RE

Army Form C. 2118.

Instructions regarding War Diaries and Intelligence Summaries are contained in F.S. Regs., Part II and the Staff Manual respectively. Title pages will be prepared in manuscript.

WAR DIARY
or
INTELLIGENCE SUMMARY.
(Erase heading not required.)

Sheet 26

Hour, Date, Place	Summary of Events and Information	Remarks and references to Appendices
YPRES. 6th April 1915.	2 Sections by day improving parapet - drains etc. 2 Sections went up in afternoon taking up explosives and to stand by to blow up any damage done to 16 Trench by charge which it was proposed to fire on account of German sounds being heard from reports of boring saps through into listening post. After investigation it was found that there were no signs of the bore. So charge was not fired. Other Sections returned to billets.	
YPRES. 7th April 1915.	2 Sections improving parapet drainage etc. Small parties repairing parapet nr. J5 Trench and installing pump and making loopholes at HOOGE. Remainder in R.E. Park. Lt. Fowle assisting O.C. Right Section in laying out support trenches.	Lt. Fowle att= HQ.- from 1/R.E.
YPRES. 8th April 1915.	2 Sections improving parapet at same positions as yesterday. Small party in HOOGE making rough. Remainder in R.E. Park. Lt. Fowle continuing yesterdays work.	
YPRES. 9th April 1915.	2 Sections improving parapets etc. as yesterday. Small party in HOUSE watersupply, revetting* Remained in R.E. Park till 12 noon. Lt. Fowle ordinary duty at same. 2 sections night work, fortifying 4 houses.	* Party is now complete. L/Atkins ill.

(73989) W4141—463. 400,000. 9/14. H.&J.Ltd. Forms/C. 2118/10.

2ND WESSEX FIELD COY RE

WAR DIARY
or
INTELLIGENCE SUMMARY.
(Erase heading not required.)

Army Form C. 2118.

Sheet 27

Instructions regarding War Diaries and Intelligence Summaries are contained in F.S. Regs., Part II and the Staff Manual respectively. Title pages will be prepared in manuscript.

Hour, Date, Place	Summary of Events and Information	Remarks and references to Appendices
YPRES. 10th April 1915.	Men [Section] in R.E. Park and watching emergency exit from villets. 1 Section extra till 1 a.m. at 2 p.m. went up & met any emergency in connection with German mine reported to have been fired in front of 6 & 7 Hants during night. Investigation showed that nothing much had happened — probably only a bomb. This section was ordered to improve parapets and put in loopholes in 22-25 trenches. 2 Section continued work in 4 Honnin.	L/C Price ill.
YPRES. 11th April 1915.	1 Section at HOOGE 2at 9 am to occupy advanced billets received in to any emergencies. 1 Section working in R.E. Park. 2 Section continued work in 4 Honnin - loopholes enlarging etc	Major Fry returned from leave.
YPRES. 12th April 1915.	1 Section to HOOGE to occupy accommodation prepared by section already there. Proceeded to extra accommodation. Set hut on to 2 Section continued night work on 4 houses. Detachment from HOOGE moving Garbutt reft with support trenches behind 13-14 also with bridge between 12-13.	New draft 47 men arrived.
YPRES. 13th April 1915.	11/Price (now his section at HOOGE) on accommodation 2nd Lieut ... arranged for working parts 100 Inf = ... worked first from from 6-2 am. 1 section making new dug outs at HOOGE and erecting bomb netting. [illegible] friendly heavy shell [illegible] making [illegible] Lipzig descending later. continued.	L/C Price fit again.

2ⁿᵈ WESSEX FIELD Coy R.E.

WAR DIARY
or
INTELLIGENCE SUMMARY.
(Erase heading not required.)

Army Form C. 2118.

Sheet 28.

Hour, Date, Place	Summary of Events and Information	Remarks and references to Appendices
13th April 1915 (continued)	2 Section R.E. Park - miscellaneous work	
YPRES. 14th April 1915.	Reports received about midnight 13th-14th that ① miners in N° 2† trench had probed through into a stove which was probably a German listening post. ② that anxious sounds of hammering had been heard within N° 17 trench. In respect of ① Major Troy - 1 section ¾ laid charge 75 lbs (a portion in own mine and tamped - 9ft dug. Fired at 9.30 a.m. Result - our trench and the German's trench crater? unless their out its surface but was invisible ‑ no damage to our parapet. On approach to German ² no signs of a lost mine. 6 holes 7ft 6 deep were put in 7 to 9 funnel to investigate. Showed that reports of mining under the trench were unreliable, so charge was not fired. One section continued wire splinter proof at HOOGE - put up hurdles and put a house in a state of defence. Two Sections in R.E. Park and miscellaneous work	* Atkins will again. × Where floor of trench was signaled to ft below ground surface.

2nd WESSEX FIELD Coy R.E.

Army Form C. 2118.

WAR DIARY
or
INTELLIGENCE SUMMARY.

SHEET 27.

(Erase heading not required.)

Instructions regarding War Diaries and Intelligence Summaries are contained in F.S. Regs., Part II and the Staff Manual respectively. Title pages will be prepared in manuscript.

Hour, Date, Place	Summary of Events and Information	Remarks and references to Appendices
YPRES. 15th April 1915.	Detachment of one draft - 20 men went to HOOGE. Bryant No 1 & 2 Section. No. 1 Section continued optical prep at HOOGE. No. 3 Section continued approach reconnoitring. No. 4 Section cutting pathway through Chemin Copse - firing up "staff" revetments (see sketch 5th April) 2 Section R.E. Park - miscellaneous work - O.R.E. admin S.O. "Log principle" shed now just to hand. Warning received for company (5th now) to move out at short notice at night - Horses harnessed.	
16th April 1915	One section in trenches in NE Corner of Shrewsbury Forest. One section continued optical prep, wiring in Armand Copse and Shrewsbury Forest. 2 Section in R.E. Park - miscellaneous work.	

2ND WESSEX FIELD Coy RE

WAR DIARY or **INTELLIGENCE SUMMARY**
(Erase heading not required.)

Army Form C. 2118.
SHEET 30

Instructions regarding War Diaries and Intelligence Summaries are contained in F.S. Regs., Part II and the Staff Manual respectively. Title pages will be prepared in manuscript.

Hour, Date, Place	Summary of Events and Information	Remarks and references to Appendices
YPRES. April 17th 15.	One Section continuing forward N.E. of SHREWSBURY FOREST (J.25.A.6.4) One section wiring in front of CLONMEL COPSE, supervising drainage & organising in front SHREWSBURY FOREST & timber &c. Two sections in YPRES miscellaneous work on R.E. Park, making panniers etc. Two sections billeted at YPRES. Two sections in advanced billets. O.C. Coy & Recent preparing suggestion for defence of Poping 2 ...ridge line round POPHO.	
YPRES April 18th 15.	Erecting trout nettings in front 19. wiring in front of CLONMEL COPSE, building frames in trench 8 for netting. Parapet also for clip on same. Ordering erection of Dressing Station in SANCTUARY WOOD improving communication. O.P. not 15.N. 82.13 & communication paths in 8 FACTORY WOOD & ARMAGH WOOD alto routes to improving communication. 2 sections at YPRES miscellaneous work. Started the enlarging of Sally Port through rampart East of YPRES. Supervising, inspecting related clearing of waste.	
YPRES. April 19th 15.	1 Section two details erecting frame clip & revetment of 2nd Revt. trench & building bridge timbers. Details building Dressing Station in SANCTUARY WOOD and improving communication. 1 section erecting bomb netting in trench & wiring round CLONMEL COPSE.	

2nd WESSEX FIELD COY RE

WAR DIARY
or
INTELLIGENCE SUMMARY.
(Erase heading not required.)

Army Form C. 2118.

SHEET 31

Hour, Date, Place	Summary of Events and Information	Remarks and references to Appendices
YPRES April 19 Cont	2 Section YPRES. making periscopes, preparing Carpenters benches for RE workshop. Cleaning up the workshop. Enlarging the entrance west of Sally Port in ramparts. The town of YPRES shelled (S.E. part).	2 Horses killed & one wounded by shell fire. P/H
YPRES 20th Ap. 1915.	1 Section - revetting and dugout in No 12 trench. Detail Supervising communications in SANCTUARY WOOD and stringing station. 1 Section working in No 22 trench and wiring in front PB trenches in CLONMEL COPSE. 2 Section enlarging Sally Port and various work in R.E. Park (making periscopes, loopholes, noticeboards and carpenter's bench.	Town of YPRES shelled intermittently by heavy artillery. No casualties in our company.
YPRES 21st Ap 1915.	1 Section revetting & enlarging dug in trenches R8 + R10 + front along in R12 +. Section similar work in R22 and wiring CLONMEL COPSE 3 Section enlarging Sally Port and work in RE Park OC reconnoitring close support line left half of B2 loop. 2nd Lt Askwith preparing maps of trenches.	P/H 1/H

2nd WESSEX FIELD COY RE

Army Form C. 2118.

WAR DIARY
or
INTELLIGENCE SUMMARY.
(Erase heading not required.)

SHEET 32

Hour, Date, Place	Summary of Events and Information	Remarks and references to Appendices
YPRES 22 April 15	1 Section wiring at CLONMEL COPSE and erecting Chevaux-de-frise for revetting parapets and jump steps in Trench 22. 1 Section also on repairs & jump steps in trenches 6 & 7. Details improving Communications in Sanctuary Wood and completing Medical Hut. 2 Section enlarging Sally Port and various work preparing material for trenches etc. "H" Section preparing map of Trenches. Capt Shearn setting out 2nd Line trenches. # OC reconnoitring close support trenches Right Half with OC LEINSTERS.	1 man wounded in Arm 1 man slightly wounded but returned to duty. Pff[r] Town heavily shelled 5.15 to 7 o'clock

2nd WESSEX F.A. COYRE

WAR DIARY
or
INTELLIGENCE SUMMARY.
(Erase heading not required.)

Army Form C. 2118.

SHEET 32

Instructions regarding War Diaries and Intelligence
Summaries are contained in F.S. Regs., Part II.
and the Staff Manual respectively. Title pages
will be prepared in manuscript.

Hour, Date, Place		Summary of Events and Information	Remarks and references to Appendices
YPRES. 20.4.15	1.30am	Received orders to proceed with 2 Sections to WIELTJE & assist- ance in putting village in a state of defence. On arrival found the infantry outside, Suppose Jo preceded to village and doubled round. Dug 20" trench N of village. Loopholed houses. N.E. of village & erected small sandbag wiring. Shelled out of village at 7 am. Retired to Grenade G.H.Q. line rearmed until 4.30pm when ordered to return YPRES.	Appendix 6 Defence of WIELTJE
		Nos 1 & 2 Sections erecting revetment & for steps Res Kb.M7. hurdles and improvised dugouts of 2 Stationary Divis.	2 men wounded
YPRES 24.4.15		3 & 4 Sections enlarging Sally Port & undertaking roads at MENIN GATE. Nos 1 & 2 Section relived at night & moved WESTHOEK. & report to O.C. 17th Coy R.E.	Captstonem left coy on leave & gone another and AH
YPRES 25.4.15		3 Coy & 2 Section night finished WESTHOEK. 3rd " enlarging Sally Port- Above & more part Mol of YPRES cross afterwards completed & Coy ordered to move POTIJZE. to bring up horses from Butt. Born under transport to POTIJZE	Town heavily shelled 3 double loot exits destroyed 1 man wounded MH

2ND WESSEX FIELD COY RE   Army Form C. 2118.

WAR DIARY
or
INTELLIGENCE SUMMARY.
(Erase heading not required.)

SHEET 34

Hour, Date, Place	Summary of Events and Information	Remarks and references to Appendices
26/4/ POT YPRES 4.30 am POTIZE	Headquarters & 2 sections moved to POTIZE ten men left in YPRES to look after Pontoon Bridge & MENIN GATE. The 2 sections resuming 2nd safety line at HOOGE & improving first line works at little Hill 60. 3rd section making dug outs for Company at POTIZE. O.C. with Major Stanley R.E. reconnoitred 2nd line switch line from Right of P.R. trench & GHQ line HOOGE	appendix 6 reference of YPRES-HOOGE 2 Canadian
27/4/15 POTIZE	3 & 4 sections constructed dug out shelters lay of C.T. & switch lines and arms made O.C. afternoon Field Coy & with Major Stanley organised infantry party on Yorkish line	2 Canadian
28/4/15 POTIZE.	2 sections at work on switch line during day under Major Ditton. 2 sections 8 pm to 3 am 29/4/15 on Yorkshire work under Major Stanley. O.C. organised infantry party of 1 Coy for improving & filling in gap in switch line.	

WAR DIARY
or
INTELLIGENCE SUMMARY.
(Erase heading not required.)

Army Form C. 2118.

APPENDIX 6
Defence of WIELTJE

Hour, Date, Place	Summary of Events and Information	Remarks and references to Appendices

2ND WESSEX FIELD COY R.E.

Army Form C. 2118.

WAR DIARY
or
INTELLIGENCE SUMMARY.
(Erase heading not required.)

SHEET 35.

Instructions regarding War Diaries and Intelligence Summaries are contained in F.S. Regs., Part II. and the Staff Manual respectively. Title pages will be prepared in manuscript.

Hour, Date, Place	Summary of Events and Information	Remarks and references to Appendices
YPRES 29-4-15 POTIJZE.	Whole Coy at work from sucked line from right of 72 Bde to HOOGE. Pt. engine too sick unfitting working party too at night to work from here	nil
POTIJZE. 30-4-15	Sappers at work on sunken line or about Col. No 3 section ordered to dig out HOOGE	nil

Copy No. ....8......

OPERATION ORDER No.21
By
Brig. General J.R.Longley, Commanding 82nd Infantry Brigade.

Reference Map
1
———
40,000

Headquarters,
1st April, 1915.

1. The Brigade and troops as under will march to YPRES on the 2nd instant:-

FIRST COLUMN:-

Officer Commanding - Lt. Col. P.R.Wood, 2/R.Irish Fusrs.

2nd R.Irish Fusiliers ....4.15 a.m.   Starting Point:-
1/Leinsters (less 1 platoon) ....4.21 a.m.
2nd Wessex Field Co. R.E. ....4.27 a.m.   Junction in ZEVECOTEN
Baggage Section of TRAIN in order of   G.35 C.
  units (under an Officer 98 Co. ASC)4.30 a.m.
Rearguard - 1 platoon 1/Leinsters.

SECOND COLUMN.

Brigade Headquarters.
1/R.Irish Regiment. 4   a.m.   Starting Point:-
2nd D.C.L.I. ....4.5 a.m.
1/Cambridgeshire Regt.(less 1 platoon) ..4.10 a.m.   Junction of REINING-
B.A.A.Section of 1st Bde. R.F.A. Ammn.).4.17 a.m.   LST and POPERINGHE
                                Col.)   Roads at MEKSEEN.
Baggage Section of TRAIN in order of
  units (under an Officer 98 Co.A.S.C)4.20 a.m.
Rearguard - 1 platoon 1/Cambridgeshire)
                                Regt.)

Route for both columns via ZEVECOTEN - OUDERDOM - VLAMERTINGHE.

2. BILLETING PARTIES. A mounted officer and two cyclist orderlies of each unit will report to the Staff Captain at Starting Point of First Column at 4 a.m., and will march at head of it.

3. On reaching YPRES, units will be shown their Headquarters and places for resting during day. Breakfasts should be served immediately on arrival.

4. Brigade proceeds to trenches night of 2nd instant. Instructions regarding relief will be issued separately.

5. Supply wagons of units will refill ~~as usual~~ on 2nd instant, ~~and follow~~ at YPRES.

Issued at ....11....... a.m.

R.Hanbury
Captain,
Brigade Major, 82nd Infantry Brigade.

Copy No. 1 Operation Order File.   7 Cambridgeshire Regt.
         2 War Diary.   8 2nd Wessex Field Co. R.E.
         3 R.Irish Regt.   9 C.A.A. Section 1st Bde. R.F.A.
         4 D.C.L.I.   10 O.C. 98 Coy. A.S.C.
         5 Royal Irish Fusiliers.
         6 Leinster Regiment.

121/5444

24th Division

2nd Wessex Field Coy RE.

Vol IV 1 – 31. 5. 16

2nd WESSEX ENGINEERS

Army Form C. 2118.
SHEET 36

WAR DIARY
or
INTELLIGENCE SUMMARY.
(Erase heading not required.)

Instructions regarding War Diaries and Intelligence Summaries are contained in F.S. Regs., Part II. and the Staff Manual respectively. Title pages will be prepared in manuscript.

Hour, Date, Place	Summary of Events and Information	Remarks and references to Appendices
HOOGE. May 1·15	Whole Coy under Major Cortley RE on switch line of superintended working party on switch line	appx
HOOGE May 2·15	Whole Coy under Major Cortley RE on switch line of superintending capacity. 1735 parties on line R1 to Sanctuary wood	appx
HOOGE May 3·15	Coy at work on 82 Bde new line awaiting Burgval. reconnoitring ground to erect Wachnican Railway troop position. Ground gradually forthcoming to new line during the night 3/4 May	appx
HOOGE May 4·15	Headquarters & 2 sections with transport returned West of YPRES to billets in grass H158. OC returned with Brigadier 82 Bde & Bullet front East of YPRES. 2 section at work building dug outs 2 sections continued work on communication trenches, strengthening & repairing wire	appx

Army Form C. 2118.

2ND WESSEX ENGINEERS

WAR DIARY
or
INTELLIGENCE SUMMARY.
(Erase heading not required.)

SHEET 37

Instructions regarding War Diaries and Intelligence Summaries are contained in F.S. Regs., Part II and the Staff Manual respectively. Title pages will be prepared in manuscript.

Hour, Date, Place	Summary of Events and Information	Remarks and references to Appendices
YPRES May 5-15	O.C. visited Hooge. Interviews with O.R.E. for supporting points. 2 advanced sections work on Communication trenches etc. in front line. 2 back sections building dug-outs.	P/R
" May 6-15	2 sections work on closer cover trenches & revetting new slopes etc. 2 back sections dug outs. O.C. visited firing line for supporting points.	P/R
May 7-15	O.C. reconnoitred G.H.Q. line. 2 forward sections at work on communication trenches support trenches & drainage. 2 back sections dug-outs. 06 Sapperwounded. Burial party 150 men on G.H.Q. line. Reinforcements from ZILLEBEKE LANE to CHATEAU	2nd Pitt joined Coy. P/R
May 8-15	1 advance section started supporting point & communication trenches on communication trenches. Supplied & cover trenches. 2 back section on G.H.Q. line revetting etc.	P/R
May 9-15	2 advanced sections on supporting point. 1 adv section with 2 O.O.b. 9th West R. & 17th Infantry digging & revetting G.H.Q. line. 2 no. back sections on G.O.C. dugout.	Lt CHASEY wounded. P/R

2ND WESSEX ENGINEERS

Army Form C. 2118.

WAR DIARY
or
INTELLIGENCE SUMMARY.
(Erase heading not required.)

SHEET 38

Instructions regarding War Diaries and Intelligence
Summaries are contained in F.S. Regs., Part II.
and the Staff Manual respectively. Title pages
will be prepared in manuscript.

Hour, Date, Place	Summary of Events and Information	Remarks and references to Appendices
YPRES May 10. 15	At work on GHQ line with CRE. Advanced section turning along found in Sanctuary Wood. 1 adv section & 2 back sections on GHQ line at night. Balance of cyclists & 70 RPOLI all trenches joined up. Support trenches started.	5 Casualties
YPRES May 11. 15	Advanced section wiring. relieved this finishing Strong points. Stormy punch from front line & Relinched line. 2 rear sections. 50 cyclists digging cover trenches on GHQ line & deepening communications trenches at T.16.a & T.22.a	1/h 1/h
YPRES May 11 — 15	Advanced section wiring Retrenched line finishing Supporting point at T.24.d.T.32.Strong pts. Rear section with 2 cyclists preparing new cover trenches & communication trenches on GHQ line at T.16.c.3.T.22.a	1/h
" May 12. 15	Advanced section improvement of retrenched line. Construction of redoubt at T.24.b. Rear sections cover trenches GHQ line. Nos 1 & 2 sections relieved 3 & 4 sections after work as advanced sections.	1/h

2 WESSEX FIELD COY RE.

Army Form C. 2118.

WAR DIARY
or
INTELLIGENCE SUMMARY.

SHEET 39

(Erase heading not required.)

Instructions regarding War Diaries and Intelligence Summaries are contained in F. S. Regs., Part II. and the Staff Manual respectively. Title pages will be prepared in manuscript.

Hour, Date, Place	Summary of Events and Information	Remarks and references to Appendices
YPRES May 13. 15"	Advanced sections, building redoubt at I 24 b. wiring retired line, putting out caps from R1 Wood & Enemy Sap. Res Section makeup knife rests and barricading road & Railway in I 10 d.	Lt Moore evac'd Hospital pH.
" May 14. 15"	At respective caps at night consultation with CRE Divn 2nd Divisional pioneers & preed out wiring galleries. Advanced section erecting breastwork of retrenched line, wiring adjoint & erecting fire step in fire trenches. Infantry digging Communication trench End of HANTON WOOD. & Supp't support line. Res Sections. makeup wire entan' knife rests and constructing machine gun emplacements with communication trenches & dugouts on road & Railway in I 10 d.	pH.
" May 15"	Advanced sections wiring & erecting retrenched line (breastwork) Called Reserve line) and carpentering carpentry parties. On support line. Res. Section constructing dug outs — at night digging new fire trench in G.H.Q. line at I.16 b. 4.4	Lt SCHULTZ joined Coy. pH.

WAR DIARY or **INTELLIGENCE SUMMARY.**
(Erase heading not required.)

Army Form C. 2118.

2 WESSEX FIELD COY RE   SHEET 40

Hour, Date, Place	Summary of Events and Information	Remarks and references to Appendices
YPRES. May 16. 15.	Advanced section wiring & revetting reserve line & superintending infantry parties on support line. Rear section & works Major JANNEY RE on G.H.Q. line. Rear section's works improving existing trenches.	It all referred to today. M&y
" May 17. 15.	Advanced section wiring & revetting reserve line & superintending infantry parties on support line. Rear sections under Major Sackay RE on G.H.Q. line	M&y
" 18. 15.	Advanced section improving reserve line & superintending infantry parties on support line. Rear section under continuation of reserve line from hill V Bn line.	It RTT refers to today. M&y
" 19. 15.	Advanced section wiring Redoubt at I 24 b trying to reset reserve line & superintending infantry party on support line & revetting communication trenches.	M&y
" 20. 15.	Advanced Section revetting trenchwork of Reserve line & superintending infantry parties, one no 1 right superintending working party for continuation of Reserve line through from I 30 a 8.8 to I 30 b 1.8. OC reconnoitred extension of support line % on left of position to join with reserve line at I 24 b 10.5.	M&y

2ND WESSEX FIELD COY R.E. Army Form C. 2118.

WAR DIARY
or
INTELLIGENCE SUMMARY.
(Erase heading not required.)

SHEET 41

Instructions regarding War Diaries and Intelligence Summaries are contained in F.S. Regs., Part II and the Staff Manual respectively. Title pages will be prepared in manuscript.

Hour, Date, Place	Summary of Events and Information	Remarks and references to Appendices
YPRES May 21st	Advanced Sections forming parapets & revetting Reserve line & drainage of same. Superintending repairs at night. Colouring Reserve line through wood at I.23.b.4.9 to I.30.b.1.8. Also Communication trench at I.30.a.6.3 and improving existing trench on line I.24 & b.1. running due West.	M.T.
" May 22nd	Drainage & revetting of Reserve & Support lines. Advanced Sections returned to Belle to at H.10.c.4.2 at 8 p.m. on relief of 3rd Div.	Thunder & open heavy cannonade. P.M.
" May 23rd	One Section at night in G.H.Q. line, wiring their gaps in entanglement and destroying support trenches. Section returned 4 a.m. 24th suffering from fumes of the German shells.	Violent cannonade. Frisbiss wounded to P.M. Engaged on 6.day leave.
" May 24th	Carpenters preparing triangles for G.H.Q. line trenches and materials for technical equipment.	Violent cannonade. Shells at 3 a.m. & later in day several near SAPPER dugouts very violent through little damage.
" May 25th	1 Section cutting & forming roadway from SAINT-PORT road west of YPRES to ELOIS DE BIENPORT NICE.	

(73989) W.4141—163. 400,000. 9/14. H.&J.Ltd. Forms/C. 2118/10.

2ND WESSEX ENGINEERS.

Army Form C. 2118.

SHEET 4 2.

WAR DIARY
or
INTELLIGENCE SUMMARY.

(Erase heading not required.)

Instructions regarding War Diaries and Intelligence Summaries are contained in F.S. Regs., Part II. and the Staff Manual respectively. Title pages will be prepared in manuscript.

Hour, Date, Place	Summary of Events and Information	Remarks and references to Appendices
May ? YPRES 26 May 1915	Carpenters making footrests. 3 men on G.O.C, M.A. dugout. Coy under orders to be ready to move.	Affey
YPRES 27 May 1915	By order of 2y Div moved at 12.45pm to ST ANDREW via ELVERD at CREUSE ST JOSEPH.	Affey
BAILLEUL 28 May 15	Under 6th Div moved at 6am to ARMENTIERES with billets at ASYLUM. Took over stores etc. from 12th Field Coy R.E.	Affey
ARMENTIERE May 29	Inspect Pegowin trench drain. R.E. ammunition. Left half of 62 Bde line. Support supervising central Lonterp parties. 1 Section joining trench between Hoppe supervising civilian making Repl parties. R.E. ammunition Repl roof of Bde H.Q.	Lt Bliss returned from leave. Capt VANE joined Coy. Affey
May 30		Affey
" 31	2 Section ump in front, new trenches group camp trench stores AC ammunition support lines at Refl. keep of Bde line Inspects supporting comm's trench instructed by 9 Div at LE TOQUET ST, DURHAM HO, etc.	Affey

Confidential

War Diary

of

2nd Wessex Field Company R.E.

from May 1st 1915 to May 31st 1915

29th Division
CONFIDENTIAL

War Diary
of
2nd Wessex Field Coy RE

From June 1st to June 30th inclusive.

Vol II

2/W ESSEX ENGINEERS.   Army Form C. 2118.

WAR DIARY
or
INTELLIGENCE SUMMARY.
(Erase heading not required.)

SHEET N° 3.

Instructions regarding War Diaries and Intelligence Summaries are contained in F.S. Regs., Part II and the Staff Manual respectively. Title pages will be prepared in manuscript.

Hour, Date, Place	Summary of Events and Information	Remarks and references to Appendices
ARMENTIERES. JUNE 1st	2 Sections wiring new trenches south of R 245. 2 " Guide slides. Details organising canteen, postin & carpentry parties.	P/H
" June 2nd	1 Section wiring. 1 " revetting new trench. Details making loom & ramp across River L.Y.S. Remainder began in workshops.	P/H
" June 3rd	1 Section wiring. 1 " revetting new fire trench. 2 " making shelter for storage of bombs et..	P/H
" June 4th	2 Sections in workshops, constructing dug-out 1 Section wiring 1 " revetting new fire trench Preparing report on Battery of ARMENTIERES 1 Section preparing frames for footbridge over River LYS (About 80 ft width)	N/K
" June 5th	1 Section preparing wire & wire entanglement 1 " mounting machine gun emplacement at FMS SE 1M MONT ANDERIS (H6585 FRM M) 1 " revetting new firing line.	P/H

WAR DIARY or INTELLIGENCE SUMMARY

Army Form C. 2118.

2nd WESSEX ENGINEERS

SHEET 44

Hour, Date, Place	Summary of Events and Information	Remarks and references to Appendices
ARMENTIERES June 6th	1 Section in trenches etc 1 " Wire entanglements 1 " preparing frames for footbridge etc 1 " making machine gun emplacements at & defence of HOBBS FARM.	eff.
" June 7	1 Section reviewing & improvement of new fire line 1 " Strong point HOBBS FARM. 2 " Trench stores Repairs to Water Supply Armentieres Making shelter from shrapnel & shrapnel proof for headquarters from muzzle.	off.

" June 8	1 Section defence of HOBBS FARM.
	1 " Revetting new line
	1 " Preparing material for footbridge & portages
	    Wire trenches.
	1 " Cutting wood fascines at HOOPLINES Bridge
	    General trench stores
	    Detail mending pumps & making machine Gun
	    platforms
		eff.

2nd WESSEX ENGINEERS

Army Form C. 2118.

SHEET No. 1

WAR DIARY
or
INTELLIGENCE SUMMARY.
(Erase heading not required.)

Instructions regarding War Diaries and Intelligence Summaries are contained in F. S. Regs., Part II and the Staff Manual respectively. Title pages will be prepared in manuscript.

Hour, Date, Place		Summary of Events and Information	Remarks and references to Appendices
ARMENTIERES June 9th	1 Section	defence Hobbs Farm	
	1 "	Wall (curtain) in approach revetting revo rue	
	1 "	Erecting bridge over Rivas LYS	
	1 "	Trench Close.	PH
June 10th	1 "	Removing fenders at TOURINES Bridge	
	1 "	Hobbs Farm defences	
	1 "	Revetting	
	1 "	Erecting Bridge over Rivas LYS.	PH
" 11th	1 "	Hobbs Farm defence	
	1 "	Bridge over Rivas LYS	
	1 "	Connecting Comm. trench at LE TOUQUET into four	
	1 "	Trench Close.	PH
" 12	1 Section	Hobbs Farm	
	1 "	Bridge over Rivas LYS	
	1 "	Revetting new fire trench	
	1 "	Trench Close	PH

(73989) W4141—463. 400,000. 9/14. H.&J.Ltd. Forms/C. 2118/10.

Army Form C. 2118.

SHEET 46

2nd WESSEX FIELD COY RE

Instructions regarding War Diaries and Intelligence Summaries are contained in F.S. Regs., Part II. and the Staff Manual respectively. Title pages will be prepared in manuscript.

WAR DIARY
or
INTELLIGENCE SUMMARY.
(Erase heading not required.)

Hour, Date, Place	Summary of Events and Information	Remarks and references to Appendices
ARMENTIERES June 13th	General overhaul R.E. & equipment Church Parade.	
June 14	1 section Hobbs farm, 1 section work at LE TOUQUET. Remaining strong carried by new explosion. 1 section being used fascines North of River. 1 " removing pickets at Houplines bridge.	pff
15	1 section Hobbs farm, 1 section LE TOUQUET, ½ section troop. ½ section removing fascines at Bridge	pff
16	1 section Chorts farm, 2 section LE TOUQUET. 1 section being used fascines	pff
17	½ section Hobbs farm & section being used new line North of River 2 sections LE TOUQUET defences. 1 " revetting at new line North of River	pff
18	1 section Hobbs farm defences 2 " Entrenching work at Le Touquet. 1 " French Ecole.	pff

2"D WESSEX ENGINEERS.

Army Form C. 2118.

WAR DIARY
or
INTELLIGENCE SUMMARY.
(Erase heading not required.)

Sheet 47.

Instructions regarding War Diaries and Intelligence Summaries are contained in F.S. Regs., Part II. and the Staff Manual respectively. Title pages will be prepared in manuscript.

Hour, Date, Place		Summary of Events and Information	Remarks and references to Appendices
ARMENTIERES June 19	1 Section at Hobbs Farm.		
	2 " Continuing at LE TOUQUET		
	1 " Dug out HOUPLINES BRIDGE & revetting river face Trench North of River.	PH
June 20	Church Parade		
	Baths		
21	1 Section continuing at Hobbs Farm.		PH
	2 " " at LE TOUQUET 2 88..r80 Canadian		
	" New Support Trench behind Support (coys)		
	1 " Building Powder Store line North of River.		
22	1 Section " Hobbs Farm.		PH
	1 " New fire Trench North of River		
	2 " Support trench behind 88..r79.		
23.	1 Section " Hobbs Farm.		PH
	1 " Fire Trench North of River		
	1 " Support Trench S 88 - S 89		
	1 " S 95.		

2nd WESSEX ENGINEERS.

WAR DIARY
or
INTELLIGENCE SUMMARY.
(Erase heading not required.)

Army Form C. 2118.
SHEET 48.

Hour, Date, Place		Summary of Events and Information	Remarks and references to Appendices
ARMENTIERES June 24	1 Section	Hotts Farm New fire trench North of River Support trench S88 & S89 S95	N.A.
" 25	1 Section 1 " 1 " 1 "	continuing at Hotts Farm Dug outs at ASYLUM. Support trench 87 & 88 & revetting Comm. " 95"	N.A.
" 26	1 Section 1 " 1 " 1 "	continuing at Horse Shoe. Dugouts at Asylum " " Support trench 88 & dugouts Support trench S.95. fire steps also supporting floors to observing station	N.A.
" 27	"	Church Parade 1 Section erecting fire steps in S.95	N.A.

Army Form C. 2118.

WAR DIARY
or
INTELLIGENCE SUMMARY.

(Erase heading not required.)

2 W ESSEX ENGINEERS   Sheet # 9

Instructions regarding War Diaries and Intelligence Summaries are contained in F.S. Regs., Part II. and the Staff Manual respectively. Title pages will be prepared in manuscript.

Hour, Date, Place	Summary of Events and Information	Remarks and references to Appendices
ARMENTIERES June 28	1 Section temp. at HOBBS FARM & troop trenches	
"	1 " Day job at Asylum	
"	1 " Revetting S 3 8	
"	1 " Revetting Parados at HOBBS FARM revetting new westward parados	P/K.
June 29	1 Section HOBBS FARM.	
"	1 " Day job Asylum	
"	1 " Strappoil trench 508	
"	1 " Covering 507 & few [illegible] & making dugout	M/t
"	1 " Parados	
June 30	1 Section HOBBS FARM	
"	1 " Raising floor of trench 580 revetting face	
"	1 " slope facing	
"	1 " Revetting Parados s 8 87	
"	1 " Revetting S 80	P/K

[signature]

27th Division
121/6390

CONFIDENTIAL

WAR DIARY

OF

2nd Wessex Field Company - Royal Engineers. T.

VOLUME VII

FROM July 1st   TO July 31st

[Stamp: HEADQUARTERS 8 AUG 1915 27th DIVISIONAL ENGINEERS] 1836

Fradmuster B.L.
O.C. 2/Wx T.

Peter Stay Major

2ND WESSEX FIELD COY R.E.   Army Form C. 2118.

WAR DIARY
or
INTELLIGENCE SUMMARY.
(Erase heading not required.)

SHEET 50

Instructions regarding War Diaries and Intelligence Summaries are contained in F.S. Regs., Part II. and the Staff Manual respectively. Title pages will be prepared in manuscript.

Hour, Date, Place	Summary of Events and Information	Remarks and references to Appendices
ARMENTIERES JULY 1ST	1 Section Strong point "HOBBS FARM"	Capt Jones Wounded
	1 " Dug outs at ASYLUM	
	1 " Support trench S.78	
	1 " Ditto S.87.	P/F
" JULY 2ND	1 Section Strong point HOBBS FARM	
	1 " Erecting Dugouts S.80 S.81.	
	1 " Support trench S.88	
	1 " Covering S.78 (communication trench) with few hands	P/F
	Supervising working Parties on Communication trench "Globe Avenue"	
	+ support point at C.22 D 4.5	
" JULY 3RD	1 section Hobbs farm	
	1 " Dugouts S.80, S.81	
	1 " Support trench S.88	
	1 " Covering communication trench into Jeu French S.87	P/F
	Supervising working Parties	
JULY 4	1 section Hobbs Farm	
	1 " Dug outs at Asylum	Slackening on Town
	1 " Support trench S.88	
	1 " in Strips.	P/F

2 WESSEX FIELD COY RE

Army Form C. 2118.

WAR DIARY
or
INTELLIGENCE SUMMARY.
(Erase heading not required.)

SHEET 57

Instructions regarding War Diaries and Intelligence Summaries are contained in F.S. Regs., Part II. and the Staff Manual respectively. Title pages will be prepared in manuscript.

Hour, Date, Place	Summary of Events and Information	Remarks and references to Appendices
ARMENTIERES July 5th	½ section dug outs at Asylum	
	1 " HORSES FARM	
	1 " a good making dug out parties	
	1 " building hutts on sheet S.68	p/f
	½ " Supervising infantry parties	
July 6th	1 section HORSES FARM	
	½ " erecting fire steps	
	½ " WELL Dug Camp	
	1 " erecting dug outs in S.67.	p/f
	1 " making dug out parties	
	1 " Supervising infantry parties	
July 7th	1 section making dug out parties	
	1½ " erecting loth	
	½ " revetting fire steps	
	½ " WELL Dug Camp	p/f
	½ " HORSES FARM.	
	½ " Supervising infantry parties in view Support line	
	S.73 – S.74	
July 8	½ section HORSES FARM	
	½ " WELL Farm Camp	
	2 " erecting dug outs & breaking up	Cookers cleaning
		house
	1 " Revetting fire steps & making dug out parties S.75 S.76 S.77 S.78 S.79 S.81	
	Supervising infantry parties at S.75, S.76 S.77 S.78 S.79 S.81 S.80 S.81 S.82.	p/f

(73989) W4141—163. 400,000. 9/14. H.&J.Ltd. Forms/C. 2118/10.

2nd WESSEX FIELD Coy RE Army Form C. 2118.

SHEET 52.

WAR DIARY
or
INTELLIGENCE SUMMARY.
(Erase heading not required.)

Hour, Date, Place	Summary of Events and Information	Remarks and references to Appendices
ARMENTIERES July 9th	1 Section on detail preparing precept & putting wells	
	3 " on dugout at revetting front line &	
	erecting dug out revetting same	
	Details working dugout & supervising infantry parties	RH
July 10th	½ Section revetting front line S.88	
	½ " " Flooring up houses near J.89.	
	½ " " Wall Centering working all pieces	
	½ " " making dug out frames	
	½ " " erecting dugouts revetting same	
	2 " " Details supervising laying out S.81 S.82 octaved & p.60	RH
July 11th	½ Section demolishing flooring up houses rear of 89.	
	Details making dug out frames. & preparing pickets	
	supervising infantry parties at S.82 S.82 Oakwood	
	S.80 S.81 . S.89.	RH
July 12th	3 sections making dug out frames fixing revetting same	
	1 " " well centering & supervising infantry parties	
	on trenches as July 11th	RH

(73989) W4141—463. 400,000. 9/14. H.&J.Ltd. Forms/C. 2118/10.

Army Form C. 2118.

2nd WESSEX FIELD CY. RE

WAR DIARY
or
INTELLIGENCE SUMMARY.
(Erase heading not required.)

SHEET 5-3

Instructions regarding War Diaries and Intelligence Summaries are contained in F.S. Regs., Part II. and the Staff Manual respectively. Title pages will be prepared in manuscript.

Hour, Date, Place	Summary of Events and Information	Remarks and references to Appendices
ARMENTIERES July 13th	3 section making & fixing dug outs. 1 " sinking wells fitting pumps, removing pumps from shelled houses. Superintending infantry & civilian working parties.	p/t.
" July 14th	3 section making & fixing dug outs & covering same. 1 section sell sinking fitting pumps repairing and supervising Infantry working Parties	p/t.
" July 15th	Handed over details of work on Brigade line to O.C. 70th Coy by O.C. R.E. Coy preparing up & standing by for orders	1 Coy on leave. p/t
" July 16th	Coy moved to ERQUINGHEM into billets H.3.D.10.3	p/t
ERQUINGHEM July 17	Erecting hut at billets at H.3.B.7.2	p/t
" 18	Beating hut shelters at H.8.C.3.4 Making & placing for shelter routes for Anzacs etc. Prepared sketch for G.O.C. dug outs. Prepared details for reconnaissance bridge at x.29.a.3.2	p/t

2ND WESSEX FIELD COY R.E.

Army Form C. 2118.

SHEET 57

WAR DIARY
or
INTELLIGENCE SUMMARY.
(Erase heading not required.)

Instructions regarding War Diaries and Intelligence Summaries are contained in F.S. Regs., Part II. and the Staff Manual respectively. Title pages will be prepared in manuscript.

Hour, Date, Place	Summary of Events and Information	Remarks and references to Appendices
ERQUINGHEM July 19th	Erecting hut shelter at H.8.c.3.4. Making moulds for concrete slabs & making but slabs. Repairing slabs at A.29.a.3.2.	P/L
" July 20th	Making dug out frames for 174 Tge.E. Erecting hut shelter at H.8.c.3.4 + H.3 + 5.5. Making moulds for concrete slabs making slab. Repairing roof of shed & jackup-up at billet. Storing shed for concrete slab making. Repairing bridge at A.29.a.3.2. 2 Carpenters with N.Z. Fd Amb.	P/L
July 21st	Erecting huts at H.3.a.5.5. Storing roof of shed at Jacky Hooung shed. Making concrete slabs. Dug out frames etc. Repairing bridge at H.29.a.3.2 & culvert at A.26.6.	P/L 11527 H.C. SMITH joined unit.
" July 22nd	Erecting hut-shelter at H.3.a.5.5 + H.2.a.3.8 Storing roof of shed at billet. Repairing bridge at H.29.a.3.2. Making concrete slabs, dug out frames, rifle batteries at	P/L

(73989) W4141—463. 400,000. 9/14. H.&J.Ltd. Forms/C. 2118/10.

2nd WESSEX FIELD COY RE

WAR DIARY
or
INTELLIGENCE SUMMARY.
(Erase heading not required.)

Army Form C. 2118.

SHEET 55

Hour, Date, Place	Summary of Events and Information	Remarks and references to Appendices
ERQUINGHEM July 23rd	Erecting huts at H.3.b.7.2; H.3a.5.5; H.2a.3.8. Making concrete slabs. 1 Dwelling floor of chalet billets.	PH
" July 24th	Erecting huts at H.2a.3.8; H.2.b.4.10; H.29.D.0.9. Making concrete slabs.	PH
" July 25	Erecting hut at H.29.D.8.7. Church Parade — Coy inspection.	PH
" July 26th	Erecting hut (shelter) at H.1.B.6.9; H.1.B.5.5; 13.25.C.9.2. Making concrete slabs, working trestles, carpenter benches, footboards, machine gun platform. 2 plans settings pieces of work at BOIS GRENIER	PH
" July 27th	Shelters at H.8.C.1.9.— H.1.B.5.5; H.1.B.6.9. B.25.C.9.2. B.25.C.3.8. Lt Blee + 12 men at BOIS GRENIER. Lt Smith reconnoitering for site for tramway from Rue de SECHE RUE Halts through BOIS GRENIER line. Reconnoitering STEENWERCK and assembly clearings. Cleaning dress at 1/4th MEE H.18.B.2.5. Making working trestles, machine gun, concrete slabs etc.	Lt Carr + 3 men to BOIS course PH

2nd WESSEX FIELD COY R.E. Army Form C. 2118.

WAR DIARY
or
INTELLIGENCE SUMMARY
(Erase heading not required.)

SHEET 58

Instructions regarding War Diaries and Intelligence Summaries are contained in F.S. Regs., Part II and the Staff Manual respectively. Title pages will be prepared in manuscript.

Hour, Date, Place	Summary of Events and Information	Remarks and references to Appendices
ERQUINGHEM. JULY 28	Hutting at H.8.c.1.9 H.1.B.6.9 B.25.c.8.4 13.26.c.5.8 At Bleu & ration at BOIS GRENIER Details making new hut, truck, machine gun traversing platform & mounting. Concrete slabs etc.	P/F
JULY 29	2 Section erecting huts at H.1.B.6.9, H.1.B.5.5 B.25.c.8.4	&/m
	2 Section at BOIS GRENIER. Details flooring old shed, making new camp etc. 3 Plat. overhauling pumps. Smith making machine gun mounting. Making concrete slabs.	P/F
JULY 30	2 Section erecting huts & shelter at H.1.13.6.9 H.1.B.5.5 B.25.c.8.4	O.C. on leave
	2 at BOIS GRENIER Carpenters flooring old shed, making well camp etc. 3 Plat. overhauling pumps. Smith making machine gun mounting. Making concrete slabs.	M/F
JULY 31st	2 Section erecting hut shelter at H.2.B.4.10 & H.1.13.6.9 H.1.B.5.5 B.25.c.8.4	
	2 at BOIS GRENIER Carpenters making well timbers, & frames for huts. Trucks for Winch Railway, Pump supports. 3 Plat. erecting pumps at Calinge Smith making machine gun mounting.	P/F

(73989) W.4141—163. 400,000. 9/14. H.&J.Ltd. Forms/C. 2118/10.

27th Division

CONFIDENTIAL

War Diary
of
2nd Wessex Field Coy. R.E.

from Aug 1st to Aug 31st inclusive.

Volume VIII

… Field Coy RE

WAR DIARY
or
INTELLIGENCE SUMMARY.
(Erase heading not required.)

Army Form C. 2118.

SHEET 37

Hour, Date, Place	Summary of Events and Information	Remarks and references to Appendices
ERQUINGHEM August 1st	2 Section erecting hut shelter at H.2.B.4.10 H.1.B.6.9 H.1.B.3.5. B.25.C.8.4 2 " at Bois Grenier Carpenter making well frames & frames for hut. Wheel truck turntable etc. & camp woodwork.	
August 2	Fitters erecting pumps at hut site. Smith making machine gun mountings making concrete slab. 2 Section erecting hut shelter as on Aug 1st 2 " at Bois Grenier Detail as on August 1st	P/t P/t
Aug 3	2 Section erecting hut shelters at H.1.B.6.9 H.1.B.3.5 B.25.C.0.4 & H.3.B.9.3 2 Section at Bois Grenier Carpenter making 4 frames & well frames Smith making machine gun mountings Fitter erecting pumps.	P/t
Aug 4	2 Section erecting hut shelter as on Aug 3 2 " at Bois Grenier Carpenter making 4 frames, Machine trucks & railway plant Fitter erecting pumps. Smith making machine gun mountings	P/t

2nd WESSEX FIELD COY. R.E.   Army Form C. 2118.

WAR DIARY
or
INTELLIGENCE SUMMARY.
(Erase heading not required.)

SHEET 58

Instructions regarding War Diaries and Intelligence Summaries are contained in F.S. Regs., Part II. and the Staff Manual respectively. Title pages will be prepared in manuscript.

Hour, Date, Place	Summary of Events and Information	Remarks and references to Appendices
ERQUINGHEM Aug 5	2 Section erecting huts at B.25-c.5-8 H 7. 13.9.1 2 " contracting specimen trench. Carpenters, making Attwlin trucks, railway plant Fitter, erecting pumps at camps Smiths, making Machine gun fittings Making cement slab	
" Aug 6	2 sections erecting shelters at 15.25"C.5-8 H 7.13.9.1 B.26.A.1.5- 2 " specimen trench. Smiths making machine gun towing ownership Fitter erecting pumps Making cement slab Carpenters Mjoiners attulin trucks + railway plant	P/H Slate produced about 200 per day P/H
" Aug 7	1 Section setting hutes at Pars G.R.N.5.R 1 " erecting huts at B 26 a.1.5" & H 3. 13.5-10 2 " specimen trenches. Carpenters A frames Attulin trucks + railway plant Smith Machine gun towing ownership	P/H P/H

2nd WESSEX FIELD Coy R.E.

WAR DIARY
or
INTELLIGENCE SUMMARY.

Army Form C. 2118.
SHEET 59.

Hour, Date, Place	Summary of Events and Information	Remarks and references to Appendices
ERQUINGHEM Aug 8th	General overhaul Equipment etc.	17th O.P. returned to duty
" Aug 9th	1½ section wood covering huts at H7.b.9.1 H.3.d.2.7 B.26.a.1.8	
	1 " BOIS GRENIER. Levelling ry. camp, trench railway BOIS GRENIER line & erecting gas dug outs at rue de POUTANDERE.	
	1 " Observation post at BOIS GRENIER.	
	½ " Debris cutting & splitting logs Carpenter making well frames, trestles, trenches Fitter overhauling pumps Civilians making reinforced concrete slabs	P/L
" Aug 10th	1½ section Revetting at H.7.13.9.1, H.3.d.7.7, B.26.A.1.5. H.2.a.3.8 & B.26.27.6.6.	
	1 " Relief La Vesee & trench Railway	
	1 " Bois Grenier work	
	½ " Observation station Bois Grenier MSR	
	" Prepared plan of Saclay for reference for Battery Establishment Carpenters, Fitters, Civilians as on Aug 9th	P/L

2 Wessex Field Coy RE

Army Form C. 2118.

SHEET 60

WAR DIARY
or
INTELLIGENCE SUMMARY.
(Erase heading not required.)

Hour, Date, Place	Summary of Events and Information	Remarks and references to Appendices
Aug 11th ERQUINGHEM	½ Section erecting huts at H.26.b.4.10 B.26.a.1.5. B.26.d.6.6. supporting trench BOIS GRENIER	
" 1 "	" F M de BOULTAIDERIS	
" ½ "	G.O.C. dug outs	
" ½ "	supporting work LA VESEE	
Detail.	Carpenters laying new floor for concrete slab, making washing troughs, jump platform for 30" range Smith repairing woodwork on carts. Fitter fixing adjusting cottage pumps.	Concrete slabs. 200 per day
		Huts
		Plan rear half BOIS GRENIER Appendix 7
		Plan La Vesee " 8
		Section plan of " 9
		G.O.C. dug outs " 10
		Detail of trenches
		Gun traversing
		Source
" 12 "	½ section erecting huts at B.26.a.6.6. H.3.a.5.5 & H.3.a.2.4	Dug out details
	½ section supporting work BOIS GRENIER La VESEE	Appendix BOIS GRENIER 11.
	" G.O.C. dug outs	
	Detail as for Aug 11th	
	Carpenters also making rifle battery.	

9th WESSEX FIELD COY RE.

Army Form C. 2118.

WAR DIARY
or
INTELLIGENCE SUMMARY.
(Erase heading not required.)

SHEET 61

Hour, Date, Place	Summary of Events and Information	Remarks and references to Appendices
ERQUINGHEM. Aug 13.	1½ sections erecting huts at H.30.5.5 H.30.2.4 H.11a.4.4 H.13.b	
	1 section supporting pomel at BOIS GRENIER	
	½ ,, ,, LA VESÉE	
	½ ,, ,, G.O.C. dug outs	
	Carpenters making washing benches, erecting stove hut, workshop w/o battery	
	Smiths making fittings for trench railway turn table.	p/f.
Aug 14	1½ section erecting huts at H.30.5.5 H.30.2.4 H.13.b H.11a.4.4 and H.13d.8.3	
"	1 Section at BOIS GRENIER	
	½ ,, ,, LA VESÉE	
	½ ,, ,, G.O.C. dug outs	
	Carpenters workshop w/o battery & H premier	
	Smiths fittings for trench railway turntable &c	p/f.

2ND ESSEX FLD COY RE   Army Form C. 2118.

WAR DIARY
or
INTELLIGENCE SUMMARY.
(Erase heading not required.)

SHEET. 62.

Instructions regarding War Diaries and Intelligence Summaries are contained in F.S. Regs., Part II and the Staff Manual respectively. Title pages will be prepared in manuscript.

Hour, Date, Place	Summary of Events and Information	Remarks and references to Appendices
ERQUINGHEM Aug 15.	Overhaul of Equipment & repaired Pumps.	PSF
Aug 16	1 Sectn repairing huts at Hrsd 0.3	
	1 " at BOIS GRENIER	
	1 " LA VESEE	
	1 " G.O.C. dug outs	
	Smiths making pin traversing mountings	
	filler repairing pumps	
	Carpenter + pavier.	
Aug 17.	1 Sect erecting huts at A.24.C.6.2	Pff
	1 " BOIS GRENIER	
	1 " La Vesee	
	1 " G.O.C dug outs	
	Details as on 16th	
Aug 18	Section Erecting Huts at H.11.6.3.6	Cement sets 300 per day
	1 " BOIS GRENIER	Pff
	1 " LA VESEE	
	1 " G.O.C dug outs	
	Details same as 16th	Pff

Army Form C. 2118.

SHEET 63

9 WESSEX FIELD COY RE

WAR DIARY
or
INTELLIGENCE SUMMARY.
(Erase heading not required.)

Instructions regarding War Diaries and Intelligence Summaries are contained in F. S. Regs., Part II and the Staff Manual respectively. Title pages will be prepared in manuscript.

Hour, Date, Place	Summary of Events and Information	Remarks and references to Appendices
FRUGINGHEM Aug 19th	1 Section hutting at H.18a H.18c	
	1 " Bois GRENIER	
	1 " LA VESEE	
	1 " G.O.C dug outs	
	Carpenters Hyners Railway plant	
	Stan repairing pumps	
	Smith machine gun emplacements	p/f
" Aug 20	1 Section erecting huts at B.25d	
	1 " Bois Grenier	
	1 " La Vesee	
	1 " G.O.C dug outs	
	Carpenters making 30ft roofing track	
	Smith machine gun emplacements	p/f
" Aug 21	1 Section BOIS GRENIER	
	1 " LA VESEE	
	1 " G.O.C dugouts	
	" fireguards & huts	
	Section making 4 panels railway track	
	Stokes gun emplacements etc	
	1 Officer & List 1 Worker See old new assembly trenches	p/f

2 WX FIELD COY R.E.

Army Form C. 2118.

WAR DIARY
or
INTELLIGENCE SUMMARY.
(Erase heading not required.)

SHEET 84

Instructions regarding War Diaries and Intelligence Summaries are contained in F.S. Regs., Part II. and the Staff Manual respectively. Title pages will be prepared in manuscript.

Hour, Date, Place.	Summary of Events and Information	Remarks and references to Appendices
ERQUINGHEM Aug 22	Batt" 'sector Overhauling Equipment & refreshed parades.	Pfft
Aug 23	1 Section Bots GRENIER 1 " LA YESEE 1 " Sor chy rets 1 " Completing road shuts at H11B H10a H15C.	
Aug 24	Organise working Conrad railway track Develop trackle camp track for on 9 mornings 1 Section Bots GRENIER 1 " LA YESEE 1 " got chy rets 1 " Leading & completing huts at B24C completing at H3a Detail as on 23rd	Pfft Pfft
Aug 25	1 Section Bots GRENIER 1 " LA YESEE 1 " Sor chy rets 1 " Completing huts at Pomin Camp Sect Details as on 23rd.	Pfft

2 Wessex Fd Coy RE

Army Form C. 2118.

WAR DIARY
or
INTELLIGENCE SUMMARY.
(Erase heading not required.)

SHEET 65

Hour, Date, Place	Summary of Events and Information	Remarks and references to Appendices
ERQUINGHEM Aug 26	1 Sect BOIS GRENIER	
	1 " LA VESEE + Railway foundations (near premier line)	
	1½ " G.O.C. dug outs	
	½ " trenching huts	
	Details making pie dish models will proceed working trenches, machine gun mountings etc L'Hallobeau for Pontoon bridge Landing stays	PH
Aug 27	1 Sect BOIS GRENIER	
	1 " LA VESEE	
	1½ " G.O.C. dug outs	
	½ " trenching huts	PH
	Detachment during down trees	
"	Details as on 26	
Aug 28.	1 Sect BOIS GRENIER	
	1 " LA VESEE	
	1½ " G.O.C. dug outs	
	½ " trenching huts	
	Details as on 26th	PH
" Aug 29.	Regimental parades. Church parade & overhaul of equipment.	PH

2 WESSEX FIELD COY R.E. Army Form C. 2118.

WAR DIARY
or
INTELLIGENCE SUMMARY.   SHEET 66
(Erase heading not required.)

Instructions regarding War Diaries and Intelligence Summaries are contained in F.S. Regs., Part II. and the Staff Manual respectively. Title pages will be prepared in manuscript.

Hour, Date, Place	Summary of Events and Information	Remarks and references to Appendices
ERQUINGHEM. Aug 30th	1 Section making huts at H.Q.a	Infantry (Lancashire) attached to make up deficiency in our establishment. Coy 34 Sappers short est. It seems impossible to secure drafts of men, work has been extremely favourably taken by the Intendants of the Division. Fifty 26 attached.
1½ "	G.O.C. dug outs RUE LANDERIE LINE	
1 "	La VESSÉE & TRENCH RAILWAY:	
½ "	Preparing landing bay for Pontoon Bridge	
1 "	afternoon erecting pontoon bridge across River Lys.	
	Carpenters making trestles, five ship trestles, road-ways, posts for Road, &c.	
	Smiths – machine gun mountings + lobby fittings.	
	Prepared statistics for type gun emplacement	
	1 Section paid Pontoon Bridge across (Rue Lys) for use of 82 Bde. or kit bridge to B. Bde. in left sector of Div. Area	
Aug 31st	2½ sections G.O.C. dug outs	
" ½ "	Setting out work at RUE FLOISRIE	
" 1 "	La VESSÉE & Railway. & bridges across dykes for new emergency roadways	
	Details in yard: Carpenters finishing turntable, make up trestle work for Bath., make up culverts sets for Roads. Trestles + table for G.O.C. dug outs & Bridge in advent for Roads. Pickets for Roads. Panels, pencils paneling rails + posts. Smiths: fittings for turntable + for punching iron plates + loop holes. Sewing, sewing Valence Concertina,	

Peter [signature]

2/Wessex R.E.

WAR DIARY
or
INTELLIGENCE SUMMARY.
(*Erase heading not required.*)

Army Form C. 2118.

APPENDIX 7

Instructions regarding War Diaries and Intelligence Summaries are contained in F. S. Regs., Part II and the Staff Manual respectively. Title pages will be prepared in manuscript.

Hour, Date, Place	Summary of Events and Information	Remarks and references to Appendices

NORTHERN HALF
"BOIS GRENIER"
SUPPORTING PT.

0 20 40 60 80 100 yds.

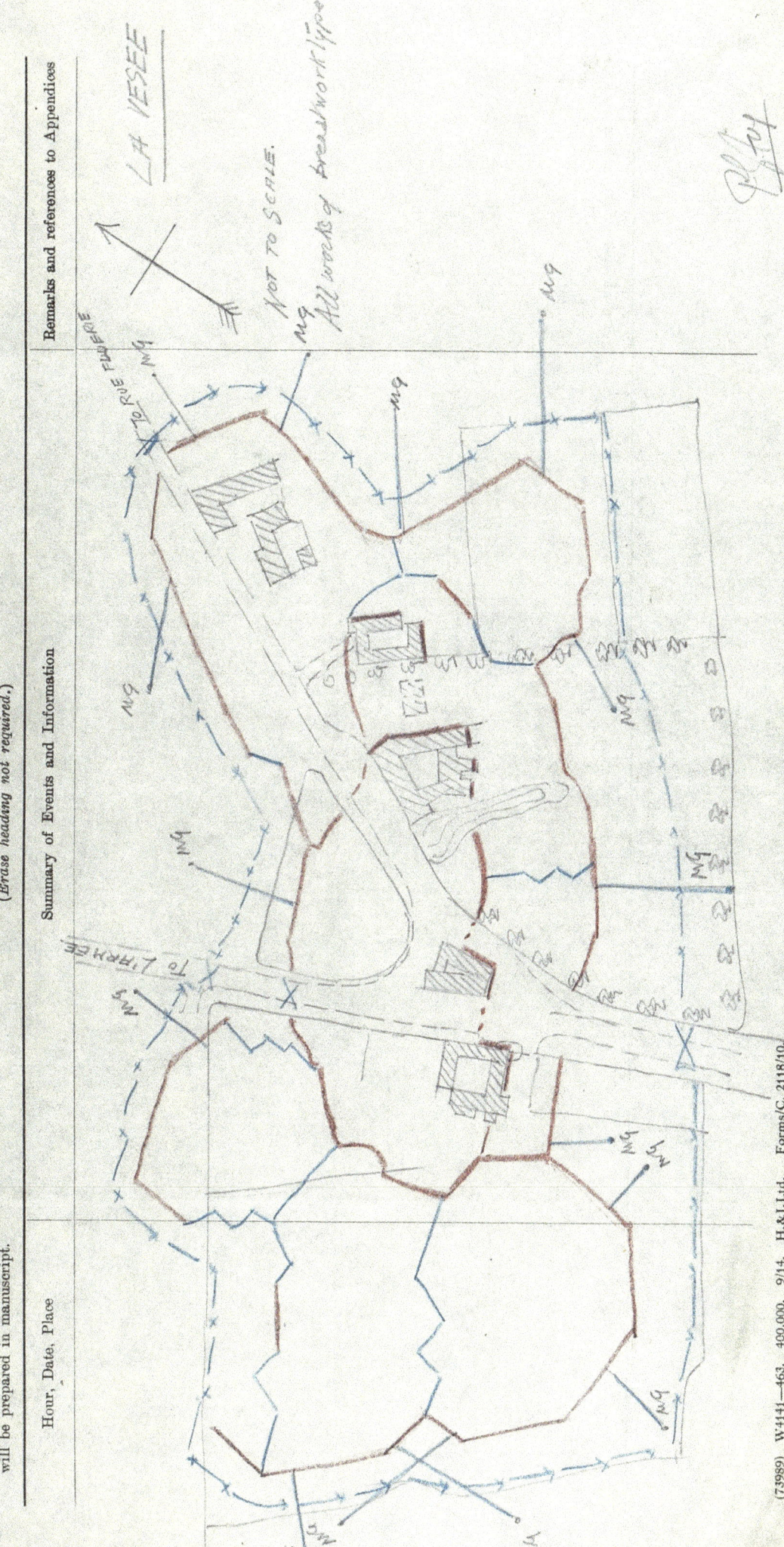

WAR DIARY or INTELLIGENCE SUMMARY

2nd WESSEX FIELD Coy RE

Army Form C. 2118.

APPENDIX No 9.

(Erase heading not required.)

Summary of Events and Information — Hour, Date, Place

Remarks and references to Appendices

Labels on section drawing:
- 3" earth
- Air space i.Q.
- Shell breaker 6" concrete & steel joists at 12" centres
- openings to allow escape of air
- Earth 1'-6"
- 7 x 2½ joists
- 6" Concrete & expanded metal.
- ½ bags
- Expanded Metal revetting.
- ½ bags
- old sleepers
- for light & vent.
- Com Trench
- Scale 1 ft per inch

Key Plan dimensions: 12' × 20' × 31' × 20' × 16'; rooms E, F, G, H, I; Conc 9 lbs

Key Plan rooms D, C, B, A (10' × 20' × 30' × 15')

Key Plan.

- A. Kitchen
- B. Mess
- C. RA & RE
- D. GOC, RA & Staff
- E. GOC
- F. GOC Staff
- G. Signallers
- H. Orderlies
- I. Servants.

2ND WESSEX FIELD CO/RE

WAR DIARY
or
INTELLIGENCE SUMMARY.
(Erase heading not required.)

Army Form C. 2118.

APPENDIX No 10.

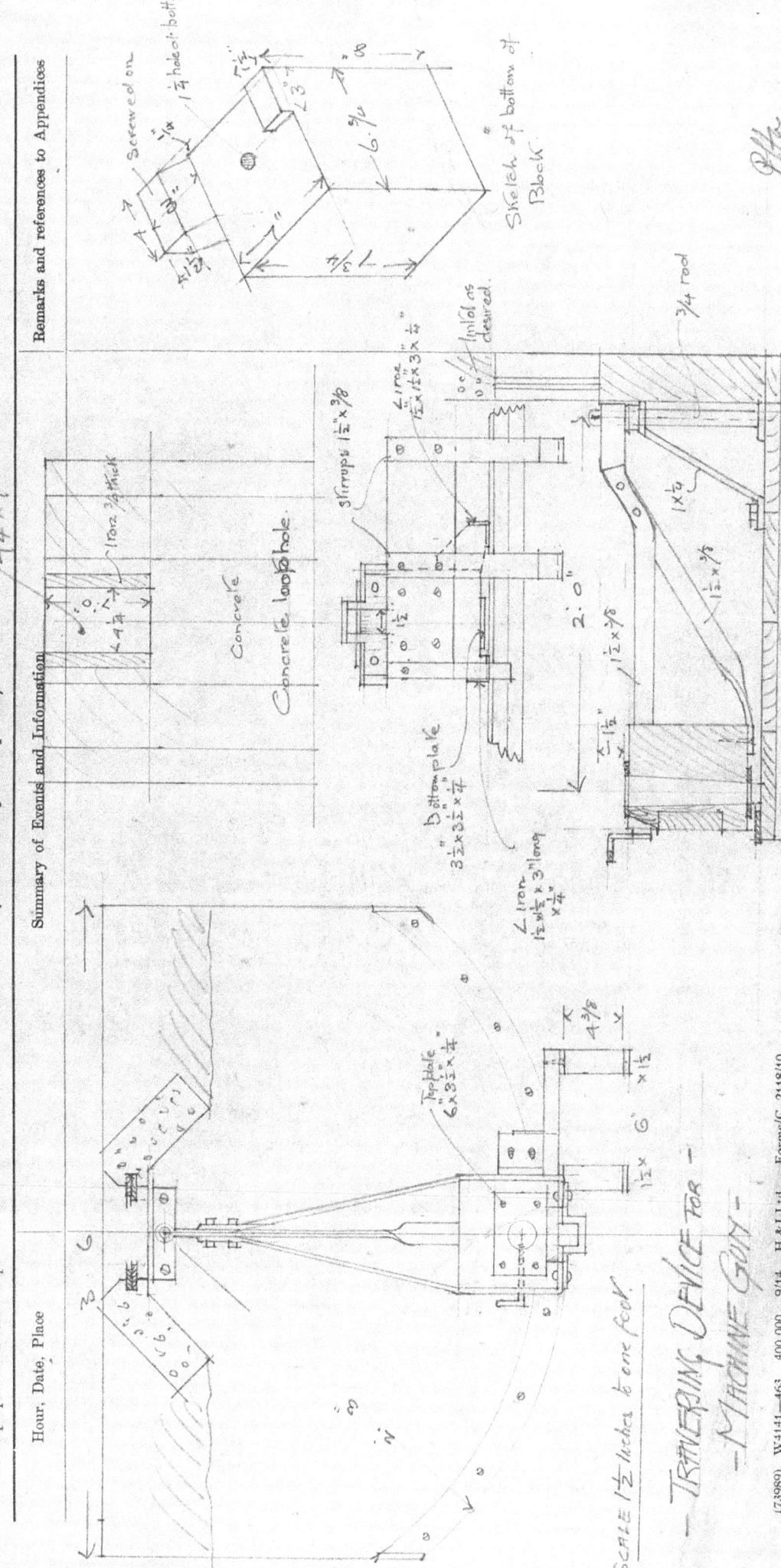

2ND WESSEX FD COY R.E.

Army Form C. 2118.

WAR DIARY
or
INTELLIGENCE SUMMARY.
(Erase heading not required.)

APPENDIX 11.

Instructions regarding War Diaries and Intelligence Summaries are contained in F.S. Regs., Part II and the Staff Manual respectively. Title pages will be prepared in manuscript.

Hour, Date, Place	Summary of Events and Information	Remarks and references to Appendices

Plan & Section of TYPE of Dug outs at BOIS GRENIER.

Scale 4 ft per Inch.

27th Division

Confidential.

War Diary

of

2nd Wessex Field Company. R.E.

from 1st Sept/15 to 30th Sept/15.

(Volume IX)

Army Form C. 2118.

2ND WESSEX FLD COY RE

WAR DIARY
or
INTELLIGENCE SUMMARY.
(Erase heading not required.)

SHEET 67

Instructions regarding War Diaries and Intelligence
Summaries are contained in F.S. Regs., Part II
and the Staff Manual respectively. Title pages
will be prepared in manuscript.

Hour, Date, Place	Summary of Events and Information	Remarks and references to Appendices
ERQUINGHEM Sept 1st	1 Section revetting trenches BOIS GRENIER Rd. revetting trenches LA VESEE Rd.	500 Infantry at night
"	" Superintending parties of workmen putting troops across ditches etc. Marking and Emergency Roads with posts at 30ft distance ? Putting in box drains & throwing bridges over ditches etc.	100 men on Railway trestling ground
½ "	Setting out work at RUE FLEURIE Rd & putting in arch pipe	100 Infantry at night
½ "	Erecting G.O.C dug out ROUMASNEE Carpenters making trestling boards, box drains, Benches for Baths. et	
South	further fitting & journals etc for Trenstalls Civilian covered slabs et	Pt Sgt

2 WESSEX FIELD COY RE

Army Form C. 2118.

WAR DIARY
or
INTELLIGENCE SUMMARY.

(Erase heading not required.)

SHEET 68

Instructions regarding War Diaries and Intelligence Summaries are contained in F.S. Regs., Part II and the Staff Manual respectively. Title pages will be prepared in manuscript.

Hour, Date, Place	Summary of Events and Information	Remarks and references to Appendices
ENGINEERS Sept 2.	1. Section revetting ch BOIS GRENIER Rd	200 Infantry day work too at night work
	2. " do at LA VESEE	200 Infantry day work.
	3. " Superintending Railway track & creating bridges for same. Making rd and Putting bridges across ditches in Emergency Road A.	100 Infantry of cov-corps one relief.
	1 " Sec dug out	
	1 " Setting out work at RUE FLEURIE and Putting in anchor pickets wire Carpenter for doing revetting frames, trap winders filler, trestles etc. Smith Machine gun traversing mounting fittings	100 Infantry at night (non work)
	1 rivework for flash logon.	B/My

(73989) W4141—463. 400,000. 9/14. H.&J.Ltd. Forms/C. 2118/10.

Army Form C. 2118.

2" ESSEX FIELD COYRE

SHEET 69

WAR DIARY
or
INTELLIGENCE SUMMARY.
(Erase heading not required.)

Instructions regarding War Diaries and Intelligence Summaries are contained in F.S. Regs., Part II. and the Staff Manual respectively. Title pages will be prepared in manuscript.

Hour, Date, Place	Summary of Events and Information	Remarks and references to Appendices
ERQUINGHEM Sept. 3.	1 Section rivetting at BOIS GRENIER Rd. ½ " " La Vesee Rd. rivetting trenches ½ " " Railway track revetting bridge anchors and sandbags revets 1 " " G.C. Dug outs 1 " " RUE FLUERIE Rd. revetting trench " cleaning up billets. Detail repairing pump at Fort Rompu making knife rests for Infantry Carpenters erecting pattern machine gun emplacement making revetting boards, etc. Smith machine gun fittings Armourer class. Concert m.g. tripods.	Infantry arrived 11.30 slept early. wet weather. No Infantry 100 Left. revetting trenches 20 Infantry Lts.

2 WESSEX FIELD COY RE

Army Form C. 2118.

WAR DIARY
or
INTELLIGENCE SUMMARY.
(Erase heading not required.)

SHEET 70

Instructions regarding War Diaries and Intelligence Summaries are contained in F.S. Regs., Part II and the Staff Manual respectively. Title pages will be prepared in manuscript.

Hour, Date, Place	Summary of Events and Information	Remarks and references to Appendices
ERQUINGHEM. Sept 4th	1 Section at BOIS GRENIER POST. sawing wood.	200 Infantry by day 500 " by night
	1 " at LA VESEE post revetting	200 Infantry in Leedoch or 500 " " revetting wires
	{ BOIS GRENIER Railway, putting in bridges. Emergency Road D putting in bridges.	100 Infantry levelling road
	1 " G.O.C. dug outs.	
	1 " Rue FLUERIE Road. revetting	20 Infantry
	recon-noitoring dugouts & rifles Detail Putting Rails et & Bridges on Two Paths from BAC ST MAUR to ERQUINGHEM and putting covers on shelters -	100 Infantry night work arrived too late to which 25 of 97th retired, could not get a message thro' prevared they would, and be-coming heavy's intervened weather
	Carpenters making truches. revetting boards etc Smith washers for fittings and repairing Painter notices. Curbour cleaning Laye BLANCHE River Making Concrete Slabs -	

R[signature]

2ND WESSEX FIELD COY.RE.

WAR DIARY
or
INTELLIGENCE SUMMARY.
(Erase heading not required.)

Army Form C. 2118.

SHEET 71.

Instructions regarding War Diaries and Intelligence Summaries are contained in F. S. Regs., Part II and the Staff Manual respectively. Title pages will be prepared in manuscript.

Hour, Date, Place	Summary of Events and Information	Remarks and references to Appendices
ERQUINGHEM. Sept 5th	Sappers superintending carpentry party revetting railway formation bed.	100 Infantry.
	Remainder of Coy was in yard on various work purposes. Instructions for the French Coy in relation to Gnrl Butts full RE refounded inspection.	No the Carpentry Parties.
ERQUINGHEM Sept 6th	1 Section out Bois GRENIER, revetting by day. Sappers superintending by night.	225de 70x + On P. lowering parapet from a morning. @ Ergingham.
	1 " " at RUE FLEURIE revetting by day. Carpenters by night.	270 Inf by day the 600 by night the
	1 " LT TESSE revetting superintending Railway. Bridging Emergency Road E.	30 Inf day " " 70 - night " "
	1 " Govt dug outs.	200 Inf. 2 reliefs of 100. 100 Inf + two (wetting (complete)
	Carpenters making tool chests, cleaning, meeting, aweling, hassocks etc.	20 Inf " two
	Smiths sharpening meetings. Artisans cleaning out LINE BRANCHES and making cement slabs.	

P. H [signature]

2ND WESSEX F.D. COY RE

WAR DIARY
or
INTELLIGENCE SUMMARY.
(Erase heading not required.)

Army Form C. 2118.

SHEET 72

Hour, Date, Place	Summary of Events and Information	Remarks and references to Appendices
ERQUINGHEM. Sept 7·15	1. Section. working Rue GRENIER Rd.	200 by day
	1. Section do Rue FEVRIER "	300 by night
	1. Section do LM TESEE " and	30 day party 70 arg/d
	erecting bridges on Bois GRENIER Railway.	200 in 2 reliefs of 100.
	1. Section G.O.C dug outs.	
	Carpenters — two relieps, work for dug outs, loop —	20 carpenters
	holes for dug outs, posts for marking roads	
	moulds for concrete slabs.	
	Smith Camp. Concrete loopholes with sheet iron	
	M.G. traversing mountings	
	Curham Concrete slabs, & concrete blocks for	
	M.G. emplacements	
	Steenwerck to LA BLANCHE.	

P. Gray Maj

2/WESSEX FIELD Coy RE.

Army Form C. 2118.

WAR DIARY
or
INTELLIGENCE SUMMARY.
(Erase heading not required.)

SHEET 73.

Hour, Date, Place	Summary of Events and Information	Remarks and references to Appendices
FROMELLES Sept. 8th	1 Section. Bois GRENIER Rd - revetting	200 Suff'y day too night
"	1 " LA VESEE Rd - revetting	200 " Inf. day in 2 reliefs of 100
	Finishing bridge on railway Bois GRENIER Line	
	Marking out revetting Bridge & Emergency Roads E	
	1 " RUE FLUERIE road	30 Inf. fag. 70 night
	1 " G.O.C. Dug outs	20 Inf. fag. 1 relief
	Carpenters making fire steps. Trestles water troughs &c	
	Painters naming Billets roads	
	Smiths M.G. loop holes	
	Ironhorn Grenade plate & Cleaning LONE BLANCHE	
Sept. 9th	1 Section Bois G. RENIER Rd, revetting	Peter Stry
"	1 " LA VESEE do - do. & marking out roads.	200 Suff'y day too night
"	1 " RUE FLUERIE Road revetting	200 " day in 2 plats of 100
"	1 " G.O.C dug outs	30 day 70 night
	Carpenters making fire steps, tethers &c	20 Suff'y - relief -
	Smiths M.G. traversing platform	55 carpenter officer attached
	Ironhorn Concrete Slabs, M. Gun cover & plate for loopholes	in site arrangements
	Cleaning out LONE BLANCHE	for all being
		Peter Stry CONCRETE LOOPHOLES
		APPENDIX 12.

2 WESSEX FIELD COY RE

Army Form C. 2118.

WAR DIARY
or
INTELLIGENCE SUMMARY.
(Erase heading not required.)

SHEET 74

Hour, Date, Place	Summary of Events and Information	Remarks and references to Appendices
FROHINGHEM. Sept 10.	2½ sections f.O.C. dug-outs	150 Inf. in Dug-up 4 10.
	½ " Bricklayer f Anaclena	
	½ " Creating paling at ERQUINF NEW Cemetery	
	½ " extension	
	½ " Details various work in yard.	
	Carpenters Tables + meeting boards	
	Smith machine for subge	
	Cement slab.	
	Curriers cleaning SOME BLANCHE.	
Sept 11	2½ sections g.O.C. dug-outs	2 Offrs eng.
	½ " Bush House headings	100 Infm 2 pelotes & 10.
	½ " Railing at Church	
	½ " details	
	Carpenters Tables meeting boards.	
	Smith machine from drainage	
	Cement slab + Nroch for Eng. Replacements	
	Curriers cleaning SOME BLANCHE	Offry

Army Form C. 2118.

APPENDIX 12.

WAR DIARY
or
INTELLIGENCE SUMMARY.
(Erase heading not required.)

2 WESSEX FIELD COY RE

Instructions regarding War Diaries and Intelligence Summaries are contained in F.S. Regs., Part II. and the Staff Manual respectively. Title pages will be prepared in manuscript.

Hour, Date, Place	Summary of Events and Information	Remarks and references to Appendices

Concrete M.G. Emplacement.

2nd WESSEX FIELD Co RE

WAR DIARY
or
INTELLIGENCE SUMMARY.
(Erase heading not required.)

Army Form C. 2118.

SHEET 75.

Hour, Date, Place	Summary of Events and Information	Remarks and references to Appendices
FROMGHEM. Sept 12	2 Sections Marching at 9 OC drop into BOULOGNE ETAPLES	30 Infantry
" "	2 " " Afternoon " "	30 Infantry
	Details repairing Wagon. Checking Equipment &c Coy paraded for Bath's at Div Baths.	R.J.H May
FROQUIGHEM Sept 13	Coy ordered to cease work & collect Kit et preparatory to moving. Handed over all details/work, plans, correspondence &c to 101st Coy R.E.	Attached duty Officer returned to Unit on duty. Lt Griss left on leave for England.
Sept 14	Coy collecting, packing & loading equipment. O.P. went round works with O.P. 101st Coy R.E.	R.J.H.M
" 15	Coy at rest.	R.J.H.M
" 16	Coy moved at 7 p.m by order of G.O.C Div to billets at IN GRENADE MARQUETTE. 1¾ miles East by 1½ miles South of HAZEBROUCK Station. Arrived at billets at 2 am 17th about 15 men fell out footsore & finished journey in wagons.	R.J.H.M

2nd WESSEX FIELD COY RE

WAR DIARY
or
INTELLIGENCE SUMMARY.
(Erase heading not required.)

Army Form C. 2118.
SHEET No 76

Instructions regarding War Diaries and Intelligence Summaries are contained in F.S. Regs., Part II and the Staff Manual respectively. Title pages will be prepared in manuscript.

Hour, Date, Place	Summary of Events and Information	Remarks and references to Appendices
TERNE LA GRAND MIRAQUETTE		
Sept. 17.	Coy fixed. Reconnoitred route for men & transport to THIENNE Station.	P.G.Fry
Sept. 18.	Coy paraded at 4.15 p.m. & then marched via Forest of NIEPPE & Canal bank to THIENNE Station. Transport marched via south end of HAZEBROUCKE, MORBECQUE, STEEN-BECQUE to THIENNE Station. Started entrainment at 9.45 p.m. Coy entrained complete by 12 midnight.	P.G.Fry
Sept. 19th	Arrived LONGUEAU Junction 12.30 p.m. RTO informed us what con. to Marg Station, after using PARIENS ordered at 1 p.m. to detrain. Coy detrained complete at 1.30 p.m. marched off at 1.45 p.m. via GLISY, BLANGY, AUBIGNY, FOUILLOY, HAMELET to VAIRE-HAMEL. Coy bivouaced at HAMEL for the night.	P.G.Fry
HAMEL Sept 20th	Left HAMEL 9.30 a.m. marched via CERISY - MORCOURT to MERICOURT & bivouaced until 4 p.m. then marched to CHUIGNOLLES into Billets. Pontoons left at MERICOURT under charge of 1st Wessex Field Coy R.E.	P.G.Fry

2ND WESSEX FIELD COY RE.

Army Form C. 2118.

WAR DIARY
or
INTELLIGENCE SUMMARY.
(Erase heading not required.)

SHEET No 77

Hour, Date, Place.	Summary of Events and Information	Remarks and references to Appendices
CHOIGNOLLES. Sept. 21	Fatigue party cleaning billets etc. Officer made tour of post & trenches on right of line	7 ORs returned from leave. Fifty
22	Started putting existing support line at 3100. 46250 into fire trench. Officer reviewed supporting trenches	Fifty
23	1 Section converting existing support line at 3310 - 46250 into fire trench. 1 Section on new retrenchment at same point & cover existing trench supposed to be moved. 2 Sections RE Park	Fifty. 1 Coy Deputy
24	1 Section converting existing trench at same trench at 3320 - 46250. 1 Section new retrench at - 3310 - 46250. 1 " " converting support trench for fire at same point 1 " RE Park.	Fifty. Fifty

2ND WESSEX FIELD COY. R.E.

Army Form C. 2118.
SHEET 78

WAR DIARY
or
INTELLIGENCE SUMMARY.
(Erase heading not required.)

Hour, Date, Place	Summary of Events and Information	Remarks and references to Appendices
CHOIGNOLES Sept 25th	1 Section new retrenchment 3310 - 46250. 1 " " support trench at corner point 1 " " revetting trench cut in banks of mine crater at 3325 - 44350. 1 " on R.E. Park.	Pty.
Sept 26	1 Section new retrenchment 3310 - 46250 1 " " support trench at retired alts 1 " " revetting trench in bank of mine crater 3325 - 44350 1 " " revetting new retrenchment at PITON Salient. Infantry party started Communication trench South of BOIS CARNIER.	Pty.
Sept 27.	1 Section new retrenchment 3310 . 46250 1 " " support trench. Retired alts 1 " " revetting trench & mine crater at 3325. 44350 1 " " revetting new retrenchment & PITON Salient Enemy blew up large mine at 3320 . 4841.100 about 5.15 p.m. no attack. Our new trenches at right on our side of crater - up with two communication trenches & traverses.	

2 WESSEX FLD Coy RE

Army Form C. 2118.

WAR DIARY
or
INTELLIGENCE SUMMARY.
(Erase heading not required.)

SHEET 79

Instructions regarding War Diaries and Intelligence
Summaries are contained in F.S. Regs., Part II.
and the Staff Manual respectively. Title pages
will be prepared in manuscript.

Hour, Date, Place	Summary of Events and Information	Remarks and references to Appendices
CHUIGNOLLES. Sept. 27 cont	Infantry parties at cutting communication trench South of BONS COMMUN	P/Jy
Sept 28.	1 Section building dug outs at FONTAINE LE CAPPY. Details started well at 30.25 - 44.75 to support front trenches. 1 Section finishing revetting of french round craters mine at 32rd - 44.35 1 Section on new retrenchment 33.10 - 46.25. 1 " " revetting trench round mine craters at 32.40 - 44.10 Infantry on communication trench South of BONS COMMUN.	P/Jy
Sept 29	1 Section dug outs at FONTAINE LE CAPY. Details on well at 30.25 - 44.75. 1 Section support trenches were retrenchment Les Poupehus revetting fire trench round mine crater at 32.40 - 44.10 ½ Section reg revetting new fire trench between the Jeanny trench	P/Jy

(73989) W.4141—463. 400,000. 9/14. H.&J.Ltd. Forms/C. 2118/10.

Army Form C. 2118.

SHEET 50

WAR DIARY
or
INTELLIGENCE SUMMARY.

(Erase heading not required.)

2nd WESSEX FIELD COY RE

Instructions regarding War Diaries and Intelligence Summaries are contained in F.S. Regs., Part II. and the Staff Manual respectively. Title pages will be prepared in manuscript.

Hour, Date, Place	Summary of Events and Information	Remarks and references to Appendices
CUINCHY Sept 30	1 Section on duty onto at FONTAINE LE CAPPY. 1 " on new trench across mine crater G.10.11.H.H.10. Headquarters & 2 sections moved to FONTAINE-LE-CAPPY and took over control of mining in PAVON-PAYAN-JEANNY sector. French Officers explained system of mines and their experiences in the area. Also their proposals for further mining. Started first galleries from F & G mines. Re-examine of the entrance of an enemy mine under Jeanny French being exploded. 2 Infantry party cutting new communication trench behind the new retrenchment in PAYAN salient.	P.R. Stokey May OC 2nd Wessex Field Co Signed A.C. M. L. Col RE CRE 27th Division 3/10/15

12/7496

27th Browns

M

1/2 Warrane P? Coy R̃G.

Dec. 15

Vol X

CONFIDENTIAL.

WAR DIARY.

of

2nd Wessex Field Company R.E.
from 1st October to 31st October 1915.

(Volume   )

[signature]
Lieut Col. R.E.
C.R.E. 27th Division.

9/11/15

2 WESSEX FIELD COY R.E.

Army Form C. 2118

WAR DIARY
or
INTELLIGENCE SUMMARY.

SHEET 81

(Erase heading not required.)

Instructions regarding War Diaries and Intelligence Summaries are contained in F. S. Regs., Part II. and the Staff Manual respectively. Title pages will be prepared in manuscript.

Place	Date	Hour	Summary of Events and Information	Remarks and references to Appendices
FONTAINE LE CAPPY	1.10.15		Started sinking chamber at F.R.1. Hydraulic keep for charge. Started shaft at point of entry R.H.F. Started Haspart F.1 & 2 head of mining Gallery. Working in reliefs of 8 hours. 24 hrs rest. 2 sections Sappers from roster of 20 Infantry mining sections attached and 16 Infantry fatigue party each relief. Also Hay Corln mining Coy attached. Lieutenan Co'l section constructing Dug outs.	D/May maps

Army Form C. 21
SHEET 82

WAR DIARY
or
INTELLIGENCE SUMMARY.
(Erase heading not required.)

Place	Date	Hour	Summary of Events and Information	Remarks and references to Appendices
FONTAINE LE CAPPY	2-10-15		Continuing shafts in F.R.1. closed F.R.2 junction F.R.4 & at F.T.2.	
"		11.70am	Enemy blew up camouflet in front of F.R.1. Magazine 3 men of this Coy. Endeavour made to reach them but gas too strong. Eventually cut air pipe and ran delivery pipe in, so as to ventilate gallery.	
		12.0	Sounds of placing charge heard in G.2. Decided to Explode camouflet G.R.2 and to get O.C. 100th Coy to explode charge in H.R.3. Arranged to explode between H.R5 pm. by electro explode both mines in series. Failed to explode mine. Cause strung out that the detonators did not explode whiche also failed. Then tried detonators direct to exploder detonators which also failed. Finally prepared fuse fuse & large commercial caps.	
		6.10pm	Lit both fuzes 6.10pm. one explosion only apparently, in G.R2. afterwards found that H.R.3 had exploded but not G.R.2 on which the Cordeau detonators had broken.	
			One section constructing bridges for camp kitchen &c. action counter sinking deep dug out	

EJM/MA

Army Form C. 2118

2nd WESSEX FIELD COY RE

SHEET 83

WAR DIARY
or
INTELLIGENCE SUMMARY.
(Erase heading not required.)

Instructions regarding War Diaries and Intelligence Summaries are contained in F. S. Regs., Part II. and the Staff Manual respectively. Title pages will be prepared in manuscript.

Place	Date	Hour	Summary of Events and Information	Remarks and references to Appendices
FOSSE 8 ½ NE CUINCHY	3.10.15		2 sections mining. Cleared gallery F.R.1 and removed bodies of 3 sappers killed by explosion Sewer Comforter. Prepared scheme for charging Exploded mine in G.R.2 which failed yesterday. Further listenings revealed enemy still working, probably at great depth. 1 section erecting chevaux aux frises etc 1 section constructing dug-outs	Офиц. моб.

2353 Wt. W2544/1454 700,000 5/15 D. D. & L. A.D.S.S./Forms/C. 2118.

WAR DIARY or INTELLIGENCE SUMMARY

Army Form C. 2118.

1 WESSEX FLD CO. R.E.

SHEET No. 54

Place	Date	Hour	Summary of Events and Information	Remarks and references to Appendices
FONTAINE LE CAPPY	4.10.16		Lowered chamber F.R.1 with 300 Kilos dynamite and 300 Kilos powder, fitted with pilots & cordon detonent to firing. Tamped with sand bags for a distance of 12 metres & then air filley. Calmer shaft T3. F1.	Fifty map.
			Started shaft in G2. 35 yds from mouth. Gun section dug into Gun section. Preparing communication trenches to start mine from.	
"	5.10.16	8.30	Found remainder of Oxy acetyl Transports mounted mines to FONTAINE LE CAPPY. Put Out Dug out of 100 by 180. Took over charge of mining in F.14.B.17 sec 45. at 12 noon. Mining operation by whole Coy per relief. Every evidence of germans filling mine near one of our galleries decided to fire charge already prepared. Charge fired at 8.10 pm. 600 Kilo dynamite & 300 Kilo powder. Charge apparently stopped German work. Enemy exploded 2 camouflets in front of our line one at 7.30 & one about 8.30 am. No damage firecastle.	Fifty map.

Army Form C. 2118.

SHEET No 75

WAR DIARY
or
INTELLIGENCE SUMMARY.

(Erase heading not required.)

2° WESSEX FIELD CoY RE.

Instructions regarding War Diaries and Intelligence Summaries are contained in F.S. Regs., Part II and the Staff Manual respectively. Title pages will be prepared in manuscript.

Place	Date	Hour	Summary of Events and Information	Remarks and references to Appendices
FANARE	5.10.15		Company on Mining operations	
LE LIPPI			Enemy exploded large mine at 9.5 pm in front of FILIPPI salient. Found by measurement to be about 30 metres distant from trench. Enemy apparently occupied crater after explosion. Eighteen extinguished all lights in FILIPPI mine and shook a good deal of rock from the roofs of galleries, and mines H & I. filled with gas.	Party H.M.
	7.10.15		Mining operations JEHANY & FILIPPI sections.	achieving radio of explosion fallenins 7m per shift of 2 reliefs. P/Hy
	8.10.15		Mining operations JEHANY & FILIPPI sections.	
	9.10.15		Mining operations JEHANY & FILIPPI section. Carried out special listening trial which seem to prove that the microphone so to detect an instrument to be entirely reliable & should be carefully used, but stolaris listened to work by ear only.	P/Hy

Army Form C. 2118

WAR DIARY
or
INTELLIGENCE SUMMARY.

(Erase heading not required.)

2/ MIDDLESEX FIELD CO. R.E.

SHEET 86

Instructions regarding War Diaries and Intelligence Summaries are contained in F. S. Regs., Part II. and the Staff Manual respectively. Title pages will be prepared in manuscript.

Place	Date	Hour	Summary of Events and Information	Remarks and references to Appendices
FONTAINE LE PORT	10/10/15		Coy on Mining operation. JEFFRY & FILIPPI (near FAY).	A/H
	11/10/15		Coy on Mining operation. do	A/H
	12/10/15		Coy on Mining operation. (do)	A/H
	13/10/15		Coy on Mining operation. do	A/H
	14/10/15		Coy on Mining operation. do	A/H
	15/10/15		Coy on Mining operation. do	A/H
	16/10/15		Coy on Mining operation. do	A/H
	17/10/15		Coy on Mining operation. do	A/H
	18/10/15		Two sections stationed at CHUIGNOLLES & LIHONS, 2 sections ordered to new camp site at FONTAINE LE CAPPY as advanced section for field works. Handed over Mining operation to 103 Coy R.E.	A/H

Army Form C. 21
SHEET 87

2nd WESSEX FD COY R E

WAR DIARY
or
INTELLIGENCE SUMMARY.
(Erase heading not required.)

Instructions regarding War Diaries and Intelligence Summaries are contained in F.S. Regs., Part II. and the Staff Manual respectively. Title pages will be prepared in manuscript.

Place	Date	Hour	Summary of Events and Information	Remarks and references to Appendices
CHUIGNOLLES	19-10-15		2 Section finishing dug-outs at FONTAINE & CAPPY	
"	20-10-15		Officer NCO's supervising working parties at night. 2 Section at rest.	appx
"	21-10-15		2 Section revetting fire steps & parapets. Attap finished making front trench	appx
"	22-10-15		2 Section revetting fire steps & parapets. 2 Section cutting brushwood making front trench.	appx
"	23-10-15		2 Section moved joined Headquarters at CHUIGNOLLES. Coy. checking equipment, preparing to move.	appx
"	24-10-15	8.30 am	Coy at rest. Coy moved to MERICOURT	appx
MERICOURT	25-10-15	9.45 am	Arrived MERICOURT & went into billets. Raining before on which. Inspection of Coy.	
	28-10-15	8.0 am	Marched out of billets by order G.O.C. Div. via MORCOURT, WARFUSEE-ABANCOURT, VILLERS-BRETONNEUX, ST NICOLAS BOVES & went into bivouac infield N.W. of BOVES.	

Army Form C. 2118

2nd WESSEX FIELD COY R.E.

Instructions regarding War Diaries and Intelligence Summaries are contained in F. S. Regs., Part II. and the Staff Manual respectively. Title pages will be prepared in manuscript.

WAR DIARY
or
INTELLIGENCE SUMMARY.
(Erase heading not required.)

SHEET 88

Place	Date	Hour	Summary of Events and Information	Remarks and references to Appendices
	26.10.15		Travel distance 13½ miles. Coy arrived intact, no one falling out. March delayed three times in front. Coy Cmdr under orders of O.C. 81st IMFTY BDE	P/H
BOVES	27.10.15	10.4 am	Coy moved by order. Cor 2nd Supply Bde via ST FUSCIEN DURY SALEUX GUIGNENCOURT BOVES SAISSEMONT with billets	P/H
SAISSEMONT	"	4.15 pm	Coy arrived SAISSEMONT. Halt made at point 1 mile West of GUIGNENCOURT to water officers horses. Roads very bad. Light grey gelding Coy felt to rear of a Cooker, 1 man too tired or excused travel for dinner & to cooked.	
"	28.10.15		Coy out rear. rifle inspection	P/H
			Draft of 39 men from 2/2 WESSEX FD arrived	P/H
	29.10.15	9.0	Inspection of new draft	
		9.30	Coy drill general out	
		11.00	Check up all stores & technical equipment	P/H
	30.10.15	9.0-	Company parade for issue of muzzle protectors.	C.D.S.D
		12.0.	Church Parade cancelled owing to bad weather	
	31.10.15	9.0	Drill 9. 10.30 am. 3.30 p.m. Troop drill by sections in turn.	C.D.S.D

Cecil M??ttles
Capt.

27th Division

121/7655

<u>Confidential</u>

<u>WAR DIARY</u>

of

2nd Wessex Field Company R.E.

from 1st November to 30th November 1915.

(<u>Volume XI</u>)

Officer i/c
A.G's Office
Base

Herewith War Diary of
2nd Wessex Field Co. R.E. for the
month of November 1915

2/10/15.

[signature]
Lieut Col R.E.
C.R.E. 27th Division

HEADQUARTERS
27th DIVISIONAL ENGINEERS
2 DEC. 1915
592

Army Form C. 2118.

WAR DIARY
or
INTELLIGENCE SUMMARY.
(Erase heading not required.)

2 MEERUT FIELD Co. R.E.

SHEET 89

Instructions regarding War Diaries and Intelligence Summaries are contained in F. S. Regs., Part II and the Staff Manual respectively. Title pages will be prepared in manuscript.

Place	Date	Hour	Summary of Events and Information	Remarks and references to Appendices
SAILLEMONT (SCAIFE)	1.11.15	—	Training	1/11/15
"	2.11.15	—	Training	2/11/15
	3.11.15		Training	3/11/15
	4.11.15		Training. 2.2 mules given in exchange for heavy draught horses	4/11/15
	5.11.15		Training. At a short hour.	5/11/15
	6.11.15		Training	6/11/15
	7.11.15		Training	7/11/15
	8.11.15		Training. Lt. Coyle to return from short leave.	8/11/15

2353 Wt. W2544/1454 700,000 5/15 D. D. & L. A.D.S.S./Forms/C. 2118.

Army Form C. 2118.

2 MEERUT FLD COY RE

SHEET NO

WAR DIARY
or
INTELLIGENCE SUMMARY.
(Erase heading not required.)

Instructions regarding War Diaries and Intelligence Summaries are contained in F. S. Regs., Part II. and the Staff Manual respectively. Title pages will be prepared in manuscript.

Place	Date	Hour	Summary of Events and Information	Remarks and references to Appendices
SASSEMONT	9/11/15		Training	D/fty
"	10/11/15		Training. O.C returned from short leave	D/fty
"	11/11/15		Training. Capt Elko & Lt Sanford on short leave	D/fty
"	12/11/15		Training.	D/fty
"	13/11/15		Training. Drew 53 mules returned 34 horses	D/fty
"	14/11/15		Training. Drew 3. Sowars R.E. wagons	D/fty
"	15/11/15		Training. Cpl Miller & Sanford returned from leave	D/fty.
"	16/11/15		Training	D/fty

2353 Wt. W2544/1454 700,000 5/15 D. D. & L. A.D.S.S./Forms/C. 2118.

2/1 WESSEX FIELD CoY RE

Army Form C. 2118

WAR DIARY
or
INTELLIGENCE SUMMARY.
(Erase heading not required.)

SHEET 91

Instructions regarding War Diaries and Intelligence Summaries are contained in F. S. Regs., Part II. and the Staff Manual respectively. Title pages will be prepared in manuscript.

Place	Date	Hour	Summary of Events and Information	Remarks and references to Appendices
SAISSEMONT	17.11.15	—	Training	2/Lt Fry
"	18.11.15		Training	2/Lt Fry
"	19.11.15		Training. Exchanged 2 Riding Horses.	2/Lt Fry
"	20.11.15		Training. 2/ Blow on short leave	2/Lt Fry
"	21.11.15		Training. Dow on Res. Lieutenant G.S.	2/Lt Fry
"	22.11.15		Training	2/Lt Fry
"	23.11.15		Training	2/Lt Fry
"	24.11.15		Training. 2/ Coy to LONGPRÉ. 2/Blow Rets from leave for entraining state.	2/Lt Fry

2353 Wt. W2544/1454 700,000 5/15 D. D. & L.   A.D.S.S./Forms/C. 2118.

Army Form C. 2118

2/WESSEX FLD COY RE

SHEET 92

WAR DIARY
or
INTELLIGENCE SUMMARY

(Erase heading not required.)

Instructions regarding War Diaries and Intelligence Summaries are contained in F. S. Regs., Part II. and the Staff Manual respectively. Title pages will be prepared in manuscript.

Place	Date	Hour	Summary of Events and Information	Remarks and references to Appendices
SAILLY-ENNONT (SOMME)	25-11-15		Training. Held 2 parades & Smoke Helmet Test	P/KY
	26-11-15		Training	P/KY
	27-11-15		Training	P/KY
	28-11-15		Training	P/KY
	29-11-15		Training	P/KY
	30-11-15		Training	P/KY

P. J. Ay Myr
Lt 2/Wx Fld Coy RE

CONFIDENTIAL

WAR DIARY
of
2ND WESSEX FIELD COY R.E. T.F.

from Dec 1st 1915 to Dec 31st 1915.

VOLUME ONE / XII

27th Div

Peter Say Cory
OC 2 Wx Fld Coy RE

Army Form C. 2118.
SHEET 93

2 WESSEX FLD COY R.E.

WAR DIARY
or
INTELLIGENCE SUMMARY.
(Erase heading not required.)

Instructions regarding War Diaries and Intelligence Summaries are contained in F. S. Regs., Part II. and the Staff Manual respectively. Title pages will be prepared in manuscript.

Place	Date	Hour	Summary of Events and Information	Remarks and references to Appendices
SAILLSEMONT SOMME	1/12/15		Training	8/12/15
	2/12/15		Training	10/12/15
	3/12/15		Training	8/12/15
	4/12/15		Training	8/12/15
	5/12/15		Training	9/12/15
	6/12/15		Coy marched out of billets at 11 am & arrived CERISY SAINT CROIX at 1 pm and went into billets	6/12/15
	7/12/15		Coy marched out of billets at 2 pm en column of route with 2 1st Wessex Field Coy to 3rd details infantry. RENDEZVOUS SP120 + SP120 + sundry papers & LONGPRÉ station arrived LONGPRÉ 6.30 pm. Started entraining entrainment completed 8.30 pm. Train left LONGPRÉ 9.30 pm	8/12/15

2353 Wt. W2544/1454. 700,000. 5/15 D. D. & L. A.D.S.S./Forms/C. 2118.

Army Form C. 2118.

2/1 ESSEX FD Coy R.E.

Sheet 94

WAR DIARY
or
INTELLIGENCE SUMMARY.
(Erase heading not required.)

Instructions regarding War Diaries and Intelligence Summaries are contained in F. S. Regs., Part II. and the Staff Manual respectively. Title pages will be prepared in manuscript.

Place	Date	Hour	Summary of Events and Information	Remarks and references to Appendices
"	8.12.15		Train journey to MARSEILLE. Good journey no casualties.	Appy.
MARSEILLE	9.12.15		Arrived MARSEILLE 6 p.m. Dock selection station. Detrainment completed 8 p.m. Coy marched to EXHIBITION Camp arriving 9.20 p.m. No arrangement made for camping space. Coy settled down at 11 p.m.	Appy.
"	10.12.15		Settling in Camp. Provided fatigue party 30 men.	Appy.
"	11.12.15		Training.	Appy.
"	12.12.15		Church Parade. Training.	Appy.
"	13.12.15		Training. Orders to move to BORELY Camp 2 p.m. Arrived 2.45 p.m.	Appy.
"	14.12.15		Training fatigue parties.	Appy.

Army Form C. 2118.

SHEET 9[?]

WAR DIARY
or
INTELLIGENCE SUMMARY.
(Erase heading not required.)

DIVISION FIELD P.O.

Instructions regarding War Diaries and Intelligence Summaries are contained in F. S. Regs., Part II and the Staff Manual respectively. Title pages will be prepared in manuscript.

Place	Date	Hour	Summary of Events and Information	Remarks and references to Appendices
MARSEILLE	17.12.15	—	C.R.E inspection 11 am	
			Leaving Camp, stores etc. supplies not draught mules	
			for Sunday rest.	8/h/y
	16.12.15		2 Coy ½ Batta. Leaving etc.	9/h/y
	17.12.15		Training - Camp fatigue	9/h/y
	18.12.15		½ Coy ½ Batta. Leaving etc.	10/h/y
	19.12.15		Training - Camp fatigue Church parade	11/h/y
	20.12.15		Camp duties, guards etc. Painting repairing pontoons & carts	12/h/y
	21.12.15		Leaving Camp fatigue "	13/h/y
	22.12.15		Leaving Camp fatigue "	14/h/y
	23.12.15		Leaving " Camp fatigue guards etc. "	15/h/y
	24.12.15		Leaving - Camp fatigue	16/h/y
	25.12.15		Holiday. Coy dinner Church parade	17/h/y
	28.12.15	—	Church parade Pontoon duties	18/h/y

2/WESSEX FIELD COY RE

Army Form C. 2118.

WAR DIARY
or
INTELLIGENCE SUMMARY.
(Erase heading not required.)

SHEET 96

Instructions regarding War Diaries and Intelligence Summaries are contained in F. S. Regs., Part II. and the Staff Manual respectively. Title pages will be prepared in manuscript.

Place	Date	Hour	Summary of Events and Information	Remarks and references to Appendices
MARSEILLES	27/12/15	—	Leaving Polygon	Appx
	28/12/15	—	Do	Appx
	29/12/15	—	Do	Appx
	30/12/15	—	Do	Appx
	31/12/15	—	Gentles Jourdain Sutton & Jacks unloaded transport	Appx
Ship			the Sapper detailed discharging same to board.	

[signature] Major
2/Wx Field Coy

2/Wessex Fld Coy RE

Appendix 1.

Strength of Company

7 Officers (one attached)
210 Rank & file including attached
1 Interpreter joined at HARVE.
79 Horses
4 Double Tool Carts
5 Limbered G.S. Wagons
2 G.S. Wagons (1 train)
2 Pontoon "
1 Trestle "
1 Water Cart

List of Officers

Major R.G. Fry
Capt. R.B.M. Wells
Lieut C.M. Wells
" Lt A. White
" Lt J.P. Moon
" Lt G. Moon
Lt C.R. Shannon R.E. (attached)

www.ingramcontent.com/pod-product-compliance
Lightning Source LLC
Chambersburg PA
CBHW051527190426
43193CB00045BA/2222